WILD ANIMALS

Reader's Digest · National Trust

Nature Notebooks

WILD ANIMALS

Published by The Reader's Digest Association Limited, London,
in association with The National Trust

WILD ANIMALS
is a Reader's Digest Publication based upon
The Reader's Digest *Nature Lover's Library*
Copyright © 1984 The Reader's Digest
Association Limited, London

First Edition
Copyright © 1987
The Reader's Digest Association Limited
25 Berkeley Square, London WIX 6AB

ISBN 0-276-40948-5

® READER'S DIGEST
is a registered trademark of
The Reader's Digest Association, Inc.
of Pleasantville, New York, USA

Typesetting by Vantage Photosetting Co.
Ltd, Eastleigh

Separations by Kera Graphics Ltd, London
and Mullis Morgan Ltd, London

Printed in Hong Kong

The cover illustration of fallow deer at
Petworth, West Sussex, was painted by
Peter Barrett

Contents

The National Trust and its work

The National Trust, a private charity founded in 1895, could be said to be the oldest conservation organisation in the country. As well as caring for historic houses, castles and gardens, it owns 500,000 acres of land throughout England, Wales and Northern Ireland. It acquired its first nature reserve, Wicken Fen, as early as 1899, and by 1910 had 13 properties of particular wildlife value. It now owns some 50 Nature Reserves, over 400 Sites of Special Scientific Interest (SSSIs) and many other properties of great interest, not only for mammals, reptiles and amphibians, but for a great range of animal and plant communities.

The National Trust for Scotland, a separate organisation but with similar aims and objectives, was established in 1931. It owns 100,000 acres, including some of the finest mountain and coastal scenery in Scotland.

An Taisce – the National Trust for Ireland – was founded in 1946 and is the leading independent environmental body in the Republic of Ireland. Like the National Trust and the National Trust for Scotland, it concerns itself with the care and conservation of the countryside. It also maintains a number of properties for research purposes and for the enjoyment of visitors.

Britain's animal fauna is a strange mixture of native species and those which have been brought here by people – intentionally or accidentally – and which have established themselves in the wild. The National Trust is primarily concerned for the conservation of native British fauna, but some of the others are welcomed too. For example changes in agricultural practices have led to the abandonment of much former pastureland, with the consequence that some downlands, with their abundance of flowers and butterflies, are now under threat from invasion by trees and shrubs. Grazing by sheep has been reintroduced in many cases, but elsewhere it is the rabbit – originally brought to Britain for its fur and meat – which is conserving these downs by keeping the turf short. Another welcome 'invader' is the fallow deer, which is an attractive addition to our wild fauna where it has escaped from deer parks.

The Trust's vast landholdings are a very valuable resource for wildlife in general. On the whole there is little that the Trust needs to do to conserve animals other than by protecting and maintaining the diversity of features in the countryside: deciduous woodlands, scrub, old pastures, hedgerows, heaths and so on. Animals such as badgers and bats are wide-ranging and use a variety of such features – naturally, they also wander and do not live only on Trust land. Others such as foxes are as at home in towns as in the countryside. A few, such as natterjack toad and smooth snake, are much more specific in their requirements and their conservation often needs close attention to management details by the Trust. Some animals are now so rare that we cannot indicate in this book exactly where they may be found.

While maintenance of habitat diversity in the countryside provides good feeding grounds for bat species, these do have specific requirements when it comes to their roost sites – roof spaces and cellars in Trust houses, ice houses in the parks, old hollow trees, caves and disused quarry drainage channels. These all need to be identified in order to ensure the bats' protection from disturbance. This protection work often involves grilling of cave and channel entrances to ensure only bats may enter, and ensuring that chemicals toxic to bats are not used when preserving roof timbers. Surveys of such sites are carried out by Trust staff, members of the voluntary Bat Groups and by the Nature Conservancy Council. The Trust's estates currently include one of the very few breeding colonies of the rare greater horseshoe bat and the largest colony of Daubenton's bat so far discovered in England. The Trust's large old houses are often located within old parkland, with lakes and ponds, and these provide excellent sites for bats, offering the combination of good roost sites and good feeding grounds.

Habitat loss, disturbance and the increased use of pesticides have been major factors in the decline of otter. Large old bankside trees provide sites for holts and places for lying-up. Trees and shrubs provide cover, marshy banks and adjoining old pastures provide good feeding habitats. Where the Trust owns river sections used by otters it can protect these features and liaise with Water Authorities to ensure that disturbance is minimised. The Trust is able to make positive contributions to the survival of other species, such as hedgehogs, for example. The pit beneath a cattle grid can appear an attractive place to forage for food to a hedgehog, and ramps need to be fitted to enable the animal to get out again. The re-establishment of coppicing in certain woods will favour dormice, as well as a wide range of other wildlife.

Much is currently being done to help rarer amphibians and reptiles. Breeding pools for natterjack toads have been dug on certain Trust properties, and these have readily been adopted by the toads. Important newt ponds are being identified and provisions made for their correct management. One of the most threatened habitats in Britain, lowland heath, is the home of the smooth snake and sand lizard. The Trust protects large areas of such

How to use this book

heaths and so plays a major part in the conservation of these reptiles. The heaths were formerly kept open by grazing and fuel-cutting, but nowadays are mostly abandoned. The Trust spends a great deal of time and effort keeping its heaths open from scrub and tree invasion. During long, hot, dry periods, the careless visitor can be a serious problem, because accidental summer fires can easily destroy the vegetation and the reptiles with it. National Trust wardens spend much extra time patrolling on summer weekends watching for fire. Fire breaks are regularly cut across the larger heathland tracts in order to limit this danger.

The work carried out by the Trust's staff and volunteers may not always be obvious, but the more observant visitor should be able to spot some of the potential problems of particular sites and see how the Trust is tackling them. The sites listed at the back of the book have been carefully selected in order to show the visitor a wide range of animal habitats, and to enable them to appreciate not only the great responsibility which the National Trust has for the conservation of animals, but also the careful management work that is required to maintain their habitats.

Keith Alexander
Conservation Adviser's Office,
The National Trust

The animal kingdom consists of all living things that are not plants. Although birds, fish and insects are therefore technically animals, in common usage the term is not generally applied to them.

This book covers most of the vertebrate (back-boned) wild animals that live on land in Britain. It therefore includes four-legged animals and also the snakes and slow-worms (which are limbless vertebrates) as well as seals, which spend part of their lives on land and part in water. It does not include vertebrates such as fish and whales, which live entirely in water, nor does it include invertebrate land animals – creatures such as slugs, snails, worms and woodlice, which have no bony skeleton.

The land animals described belong to one or the other of three major groups: mammals, amphibians or reptiles, which have each evolved different ways of using energy and reproducing their kind. Of the world's 5,000 species of mammals, only about 60 wild species live in mainland Britain – even fewer in Ireland. The exact number of species is sometimes difficult to establish because some are rare and nocturnal and therefore hard to identify, especially bats. There are only six species of British reptiles – three snakes and three lizards out of a worldwide total of more than 3,000. Many of these wild animals may be seen on the properties owned by the National Trust in Britain and Northern Ireland, The National Trust for Scotland and An Taisce in the Republic of Ireland.

In the field guide section (pages 8–95), you will find Sites Guide boxes, containing a brief description of each species, together with an indication of where they may be seen. In some instances, this note is followed by a sequence of numbers. These simply direct you to sites (on pages 98–123) where you may see the species concerned. Opening times and admission fees were correct at the time of going to press, but may subsequently have changed slightly. Many National Trust properties comprise an historic house and grounds. Prices given generally refer to admission to both house and grounds, but in some cases special arrangements are available for those who wish to enter the grounds for natural history purposes.

The 'notebook' panels
At the foot of each species entry you will find a blank panel for making your own notes and sketches. Making records of field observations enables you to identify the features of a species more easily as well as making an enjoyable diary of your field trips. Use the panel for sketches as well as notes.

Using the maps
Distribution maps are given for each of the wild species featured in the book, and are based on the best and most up-to-date surveys. On each map, the area coloured in green is the area of country where the species can be reasonably expected to be found within its preferred habitat, which is indicated in the caption below.

For example, the brown hare will be found mainly in open fields in the green area. The grey squirrel is likely to be absent from quite large stretches of moorland within the green area on the map, but they are too small to be indicated.

Badgers use trees near the sett to sharpen their claws and clean mud off their paws, particularly on heavy soils. They prefer rough-barked trees such as elders and oaks.

Straw, dry leaves, bracken or green plants are used as bedding. The badger gathers them between forepaws and chin and shuffles backwards to the sett entrance.

Badgers keep to the same well-beaten paths through their territory. Wiry black-and-white hairs on a fence indicate a badger route. To prevent badgers tearing up rabbit-proof fencing, forestry fences may have special badger gates with heavy flaps.

In some urban areas, badgers will enter gardens to feed on household scraps, crops, windfall fruit or dustbin refuse, and may do damage.

Badgers belonging to the same group scent each other to aid recognition, a process known as musking. A musking badger backs on to another with its tail raised to secrete an odorous liquid from a gland under the tail.

Notes and Sketches

White-tipped
ears

Striped
head

Strong
forepaws

The badger emerges cautiously from
its burrow (or sett), sniffing for danger,
soon after dusk. Its black-and-white
striped head with small, white-tipped
ears, is distinctive. Strong forepaws
with long claws make it a powerful
digger. Male 30 in. (76 cm) head and
body; 6 in. (15 cm) tail. Female smaller.

Commonest in south and west.
Scarce in East Anglia, parts of
Scotland, urban Midlands.

Sites Guide

Badgers are powerful
diggers and the huge piles of
soil found outside their setts
are a sure sign of badgers at
work. Badgers occur
throughout most of the
British Isles and have been
recorded at 3, 5, 8, 11–14,
16, 19, 21–24, 27–38, 41–
43, 45, 49, 52–55, 57, 58,
62, 67, 69, 70.

Badger *Meles meles*

There are badgers in most parts of the country, and some places
have been named after them, such as Brockhall in Northamp-
tonshire – *brocc* being Old English for badger. Some inhabit
urban areas, notably on the south coast and in Essex, London,
Bath and Bristol. Generally they are active at night and rarely
seen. Badgers live in extensive burrow systems, or setts, dug out
with their broad, powerful forepaws. Setts are usually in woodland, sometimes in fields or rubbish dumps, and include sleep-
ing chambers where there is regularly changed bedding. Each
sett is occupied by a group of one or two families. The group
forages within an established territory, defended against outsid-
ers, which has well-defined paths between the sett, feeding
grounds and latrines – dung pits dug singly or in groups.

Earthworms are the badger's main food, supplemented by
cereals, beetles, fruit in autumn, and some mammals, particularly young rabbits dug out from their burrows. Badgers will also
dig out and eat the contents of wasp and bee nests. A few badgers
probably survive for about 15 years. Unauthorised killing is
illegal, but because badgers may be infecting cows with tuber-
culosis in certain areas, there has been official gassing.

Notes and Sketches

The home and habits of a badger community

A badger community usually includes a number of adult boars and sows and one or two litters of cubs, up to 15 animals in all. Setts are often dug in sloping ground or under a rocky overhang, and are generally in woods or copses. Large setts may have more than 40 entrances and have been used for decades by generations of badgers.

There is usually one main sett and a number of outlying setts distributed around the territory. The main sett is a network of tunnels and chambers on several levels, usually within about 40 in. (100 cm) of the surface. Entrance holes are about 12 in. (30 cm) wide. Territories vary in size, but may be 100–125 acres (40–50 hectares) in extent.

Badgers mate between February and October, but the peak season is in spring. However, implantation of the fertilised egg is delayed until December and cubs are born from mid-January to mid-March, usually two or three in a litter. They are covered with a silky, greyish-white fur and are blind until about five weeks old. Weaning starts at 12 weeks old. Some cubs stay with the family group, others leave to find new territories and may move long distances to do so. Most of the cubs that leave do not go until their first winter, but some go in late summer when only a few months old.

In autumn, badgers lay down a large amount of fat under their skin, increasing their weight by up to 60 per cent. They do not hibernate, but from mid-December to mid-February activity is reduced and they live mainly off their fat.

Badgers often play together and groom each other. Mutual grooming may involve two badgers or several.

Elder bushes and nettles often grow near setts. Badgers eat elderberries and disperse seeds in their droppings. Soil enriched with dung favours elder and nettle growth.

Fallen trees near the sett provide both a playground and a food source. Badgers like to climb along them and to extract beetles, slugs and snails from under rotting bark.

Notes and Sketches

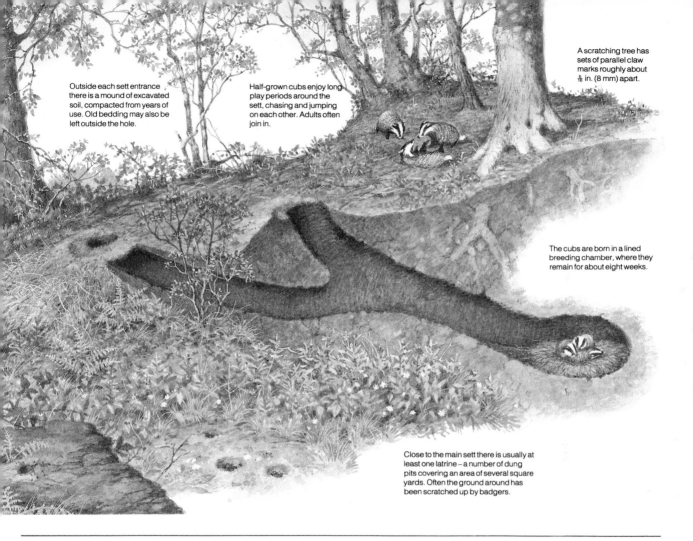

Outside each sett entrance there is a mound of excavated soil, compacted from years of use. Old bedding may also be left outside the hole.

Half-grown cubs enjoy long play periods around the sett, chasing and jumping on each other. Adults often join in.

A scratching tree has sets of parallel claw marks roughly about ⅜ in. (8 mm) apart.

The cubs are born in a lined breeding chamber, where they remain for about eight weeks.

Close to the main sett there is usually at least one latrine – a number of dung pits covering an area of several square yards. Often the ground around has been scratched up by badgers.

Notes and Sketches

Surplus food is often buried for later, but another fox in the family group may find it first. The fox uses its forefeet to dig a hole, its nose to push soil over the cache.

Prey such as voles may be detected by sound. The fox leaps on the spot the sound came from, pinning the prey with its forepaws.

About May foxes begin to moult their winter coats, and scratch to remove loose fur. The moult spreads slowly along the back and hindquarters and they look rather untidy for most of the summer.

Foxes can climb well. They will use the lower branches of a tree as a daytime resting place that also serves as a good vantage point.

Although foxes from the same group forage alone, they may meet during the night for play or mutual grooming. They greet each other with wagging tails and whickering noises.

Notes and Sketches

Amber eyes

Bushy tail

The fox's amber eyes and bushy tail are distinctive. Its coat may vary from yellow-brown to red-brown, and its rump is often silvery with white-tipped hairs. The lower legs and the backs of the ears are black, the tail-tip often white. Dog 26 in. (66 cm) head and body, 15 in. (38 cm) tail. Vixen smaller.

Widespread and abundant in many habitats, ranging from city streets to mountains.

SITES GUIDE

Foxes are good climbers and may spend the day in the lower branches of trees from where they can easily spot the approach of danger. In towns they put this ability to good use and often seek safety on the roofs of garages during the day. These mammals are very widespread and occur at almost all the sites in this book.

Fox *Vulpes vulpes*

Many tales are told of the cunning of the fox in eluding the hunt or catching prey. Foxes are indeed resourceful animals, and manage to thrive in all sorts of places. They are mostly active at night, when they forage for whatever food is available, scavenging from carcasses or killing small mammals, especially field voles and rabbits. In summer they catch large numbers of beetles, and in autumn feed on fruit. Foxes in coastal areas forage along the shore for crabs and dead fish or seabirds.

Alert and wary, foxes have acute hearing and a keen sense of smell. Their eyes are quick to detect movement but do not see stationary objects so well. A fox looks its best from October to January when its coat is full and thick. For most of the summer it undergoes a protracted moult. Although foxes are normally seen alone, they live in family groups usually made up of a dog fox (male), a breeding vixen (female) and her cubs, and perhaps one or two non-breeding vixens from previous litters. A den or earth is used at breeding time. A den may be in a rock crevice or under tree roots. The vixen may dig her own earth or enlarge an abandoned burrow. At other times, foxes usually shelter above ground. Few live more than eight years.

Notes and Sketches

Rearing a family of fox cubs

Foxes breed only once a year. The mating season lasts from Christmas until about February, when courting foxes may be heard emitting short triple barks, or may shatter the silence of the night with unearthly screams as a vixen calls to a potential mate. The dog fox and vixen hunt and travel together for about three weeks. Towards the end of this period they may mate several times. The vixen is pregnant for about 53 days, the peak period for births being around mid–March.

A litter of cubs is born on the bare soil of the den or earth; the vixen makes no nest. The cubs open their eyes when 10–14 days old, and take their first solid food – often regurgitated by their mother – when they are from three to four weeks old. A week later they emerge from the den for the first time, and their dark brown cub coats start to change colour. By about eight weeks the coat is red-brown. Non-breeding vixens may help to rear the cubs. Throughout summer the cubs stay together as a family, reaching adult size about September. Young vixens may stay with the family group, but young dog foxes leave in autumn or winter to find their own territories. At this time many young foxes are killed by cars, foxhounds or for their pelts.

During the mating season the dog fox, tail held straight out, will follow the vixen for long periods. They may be seen during the daytime.

Four-week-old cub

A litter of four or five round-faced, short-eared cubs is born in March or April. They are born blind and are covered with fur of a deep chocolate brown.

Cubs grow rapidly. At four or five weeks old their blue eyes slowly change to amber and their coats begin to go reddish-brown.

Eight-week-old cub

Notes and Sketches

If disturbed, the vixen moves the cubs to another earth. Cubs up to six weeks old are carried in her mouth, one at a time, each held by the scruff of the neck.

At the end of the year, some of the cubs leave to find their own territories. An adult will sometimes drive a young fox away from the group.

The vixen stays in the den or earth with her cubs until they are two weeks old, the dog fox bringing her food. After that she spends more time outside.

As the cubs grow up, they fight and squabble more and more often. Sparring cubs will stand on their hind legs and push each other.

Notes and Sketches

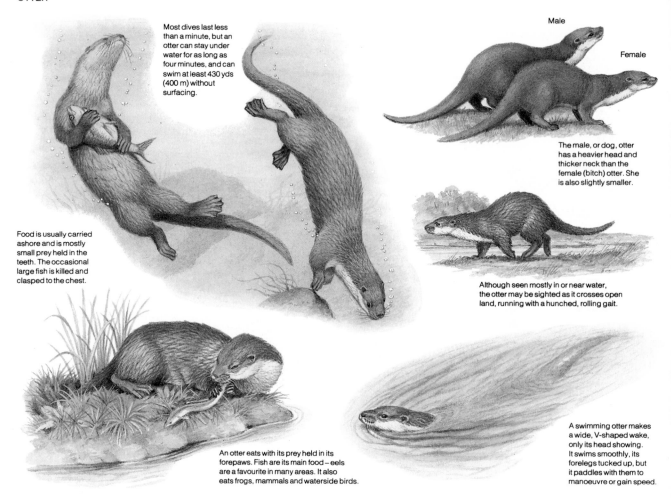

Most dives last less than a minute, but an otter can stay under water for as long as four minutes, and can swim at least 430 yds (400 m) without surfacing.

Male

Female

The male, or dog, otter has a heavier head and thicker neck than the female (bitch) otter. She is also slightly smaller.

Food is usually carried ashore and is mostly small prey held in the teeth. The occasional large fish is killed and clasped to the chest.

Although seen mostly in or near water, the otter may be sighted as it crosses open land, running with a hunched, rolling gait.

An otter eats with its prey held in its forepaws. Fish are its main food – eels are a favourite in many areas. It also eats frogs, mammals and waterside birds.

A swimming otter makes a wide, V-shaped wake, only its head showing. It swims smoothly, its forelegs tucked up, but it paddles with them to manoeuvre or gain speed.

Notes and Sketches

Small ears

Streamlined for speed in the water, the otter has small ears, a long body with a powerful, tapering tail and short, strong legs with webbed feet. It often stands upright to look around, balancing on its hind feet and tail. Male 36 in. (90 cm) head and body, 16 in. (40 cm) tail.

Ears, eyes and nostrils set well to the top of the otter's head aid surface swimming. Its broad, flat head helps to distinguish it from a mink.

Declining except in parts of Scotland. Rare or absent in much of Midlands, south.

Thick, tapered tail

Webbed feet

Sites Guide

Pesticides, river canalisation, hunting and disturbance have all contributed to the virtual disappearance of the otter from England and its scarcity in Wales. However, Irish and Scottish numbers are still fairly high and you may see their signs here, or even one swimming. Otters are now protected.

Otter *Lutra lutra*

Few people ever see a wild otter in Britain. Otters are rare today, but until the 1950s could be found throughout most of the country. Since then numbers have declined rapidly. Even where they do occur, it is more usual to see an otter's droppings than the animal itself, except perhaps on Scotland's west coast.

Otters live by undisturbed waters where there is plenty of cover, mostly by freshwater lakes, rivers, or quite small streams as well as some coasts. Fish are their main food. Strong swimmers, as much at home in the water as on land, otters have large lungs that aid underwater swimming. When diving they can slow down oxygen consumption by reducing their heartbeats. They can focus their eyes to see as well under water as on the surface and have a moustache of stiff whiskers to help them feel their way at the bottom of a muddy stream or in the dark; it may also help in detecting prey.

No one knows for certain how long otters live in the wild, but captive otters have lived to be 20. Man has been the otter's chief enemy, through hunting for sport and killing for fur or for fish protection. Otters are now protected by law, and attempts are being made to conserve the remaining otter population.

Notes and Sketches

The pine marten is one of the few predators agile enough to catch a squirrel. If it falls, its lithe body twists to land safely on all fours from as high as 65 ft (20 m).

Food is obtained mostly on the ground and consists mainly of small birds and mammals which it seeks out by sight and smell. It also eats beetles, caterpillars, carrion, eggs and lots of berries.

The marten climbs trees with ease. It grasps the trunk firmly, digs in its claws, and uses both hind legs together to force itself upwards in a series of jerky movements.

Active mainly at night, the pine marten is rarely seen in daylight. It may be glimpsed as it crosses an open space such as a forest ride, and recognised by its distinctive bounding gait and bushy tail.

Although it can swim, the marten prefers not to. It leaps from stone to stone to cross a mountain stream.

Notes and Sketches

Male

Female

Creamy-yellow throat

Found in remote areas, but it is spreading into new forest plantations.

The pine marten, alert and elusive, is cat-size, with noticeably long rich brown fur and a bushy tail. Its conspicuous creamy-yellow throat is distinctive. Male 18 in. (45 cm) head and body, 9 in. (23 cm) tail. Female slightly smaller.

Pine marten *Martes martes*

Once the lithe pine marten was widespread in Britain. Now it is uncommon, found mainly in remote forests or sometimes on rocky moorland where it spends quite a lot of time on the ground looking for food in forest rides and grassy areas. Trapping for its rich fur and persecution by gamekeepers led to its decline over the past 200 years, although it was never a serious threat to game birds. Felling of forests has also reduced its numbers, but today new plantations offer it a chance of expansion.

Pine martens breed only once a year, mating in July or August. But there is a delay in the implantation of the fertilised egg, and females do not become pregnant until about January. A litter averages three babies, born in March or April in a den usually in a crevice among rocks or tree roots. The young spend at least six weeks in the den before their eyes open and they are big enough to venture out, and the family stays together until they are six months old. Youngsters grow quickly, reaching adult size in their first summer, but until their first winter moult they have paler, woollier fur than adults. Apart from man, the pine marten has no serious enemies and can expect to live for several years – some may reach ten or more.

Notes and Sketches

Dark
guard hairs

Dark
mask

Sites Guide

Although confined to Wales in recent years, the polecat is beginning to spread across the border into England. Polecats feed mainly on small mammals or reptiles but they have been known to kill animals as large as a hare. Look for signs of polecats at the sites in Wales and the Marches, particularly 26, 29, 48.

Polecat *Mustela putorius*

Only in central and western Wales did the polecat survive the centuries of persecution that led to its near extinction in Britain. Once known as the foul-mart because of its strong smell, it used to be widespread, but was ruthlessly trapped and killed for its fur (known as fitch) and because it was considered a threat to game and livestock. Since the 1950s trapping has declined and numbers seem to be increasing, but the picture is confused by the numbers of ferrets living wild in many parts.

Ferrets are creamy-white, domesticated polecats used to catch rabbits, and some escape or are lost. Over generations, many have reverted to polecat colouring and are known as polecat-ferrets; there are established colonies in many counties, and they have also interbred with the spreading population of true polecats. So polecats tend to vary in colour because their long outer (guard) hairs may range from creamy-yellow to almost black, depending on how much ferret and how much true polecat is in their ancestry. Polecats are commonest on farmland, and are mostly active at night. They often inhabit abandoned rabbit burrows. Some live to be five or more. They have few natural predators but are often killed by cars.

The polecat has creamy-yellow woolly underfur protected by long, dark guard hairs, and may vary in colour from pale to almost black. A polecat-ferret looks similar, but its face markings differ. Male 15 in. (38 cm) head and body, 5½ in. (14 cm) tail.

Found mainly in Wales but spreading. Polecat-ferrets found throughout Britain.

Polecat

Polecat-ferret

Ferret

A polecat has white ear tips and a dark mask. A polecat-ferret usually has a paler forehead and no mask. A pure ferret is creamy-white.

Notes and Sketches

Chocolate-brown fur

Rarely seen far from a river or lake, the mink is mostly active at night, often preying on waterfowl. Its dense, glossy, chocolate-brown fur looks almost black from a distance, when wet especially. Male 16 in. (40 cm) head and body, 5 in. (12.5 cm) tail. Female usually smaller.

A waterside animal becoming steadily more numerous and still extending its range.

SITES GUIDE

Despite the fact that they are markedly different in size and colour, many people mistake mink for otters. The mink is much smaller – about the size of a small cat – and is darker than the otter. With the exception of Scotland, it is much more likely to be seen during the day. Mink may be seen at 3, 8, 15, 25, 26, 29, 32, 47, 49, 50, 51, 62, 65, 67.

Mink *Mustela vison*

When the mink was introduced to Britain from North America in the late 1920s, it was intended to be kept captive on fur farms and raised for its valuable pelt. But many farms had inadequate fences, and as mink are good climbers many escaped and bred in the wild. Since 1930 they have spread over most of Britain.

At first mink were assumed to be a pest and attempts were made to get rid of the wild population. Thousands were trapped, but with little noticeable effect. The mink now appears to be a permanent addition to Britain's wildlife, with few threats to its continued existence. At a time when many British mammals are becoming rare, a successful newcomer might seem a welcome addition, but there is still controversy over the mink's acceptability. Mink eat a lot of fish, and their depredations among trout on a fish farm or valuable young salmon can be serious. They will also eat water birds and nestlings. Although mink probably do not seriously compete with otters for food, they may prevent otters from recolonising suitable habitats. Young mink are born in a den among waterside stones or tree roots. From June onwards they can be seen foraging with their mother, and are fully grown by autumn.

Notes and Sketches

*Creamy-white
underparts*

The stoat often kills prey more
than twice its own size by biting
deeply into the neck. Rabbits,
small mammals and birds
provide the bulk of its diet.

*Black
tail-tip*

Alert and inquisitive, the stoat
often sits upright to view its
surroundings, revealing the
sharp division between its
creamy-white underside and
brown flanks. Its black tail-tip is
distinctive. Male about 10 in.
(25 cm) head and body, 3 in.
(76 mm) or more tail.

Widespread in woods, farms,
uplands, despite extensive
trapping and shooting.

SITES GUIDE

One of the characteristics for
which the stoat is well
known is the ability to moult
to a white winter coat in
areas with prolonged snow,
such as the north of
Scotland. Even then,
however, it still retains the
black tip of its tail. Stoats
may be seen at most of the
sites in this book.

Stoat *Mustela erminea*

Slim and savage, the stoat is one of the fiercest of predators,
active by day or night. It relentlessly tracks down its prey by
scent, and its habit of sometimes licking blood from its victim's
fur has given rise to the legend that it sucks blood.

Although the stoat has suffered extensively at the hands of
gamekeepers, it has remained widely distributed and numerous.
The biggest threat to its existence was the introduction of
myxomatosis in the 1950s, the disease that wiped out almost all
the rabbit population. But as the stoat eats many other things
beside rabbits, even occasional insects, it was able to survive in
most parts. A stoat's hunting ground usually covers about 50
acres (20 hectares). Its den is in a rock crevice or abandoned
rabbit burrow, and it normally lives alone. Stoats mate in
summer, but implantation of the fertilised egg is delayed until
the following March, females giving birth in April or May.
Young stoats, independent at about ten weeks old, may be
mistaken for weasels but can be recognised by the black tail-tip.

In Ireland, stoats are darker and, like weasels, have a wavy
dividing line between flank and belly fur. As there are no
weasels in Ireland, there is no problem with recognition.

Notes and Sketches

Brown tail

Wavy flank line

The weasel's brown fur meets its white underparts in an irregular line along its flanks, and there are small brown patches on its throat. Its tail is brown to the tip. Unlike the stoat, its coat does not go white in winter. Male about 8 in. (20 cm) head and body, 2 in. (50 mm) tail. Female slightly smaller.

Brown throat-patch

Widespread in most habitats, but absent from Ireland and many of the smaller islands.

A weasel is most likely to be seen as it streaks across a road, its slim body fully stretched and its short legs moving so fast they blur.

Sites Guide

The weasel's very slim body is of enormous value when it is hunting prey like mice and voles because it can pursue them down their tunnels. Weasels are also known to raid bird nesting boxes, slipping easily through the entrance hole. Weasels may be seen at almost every site in Britain but they do not occur in Ireland.

Weasel *Mustela nivalis*

The weasel looks something like a long, slim, fast-moving mouse, and often moves in undulating bounds of 12 in. (30 cm). It is the smallest British carnivore, and a fierce hunter by day or night. Mice are one of its main foods – one weasel may eat hundreds in a year, so farmers and foresters should regard it as a friend. Each weasel has a territory of 10–20 acres (4–8 hectares), females using much smaller ones than males. Territory size depends on the food available; where there is plenty there is no need to hunt so far afield. A weasel eats roughly 1 oz (28 g) of food a day – about 25 per cent of its own weight.

Young weasels are born in April or May, and there may be a second litter in July or August. Youngsters stay with the mother, often hunting in family parties, until up to 12 weeks old. By this time they are fully grown. Unlike other British carnivores, which do not breed in their first year, young weasels may be capable of breeding during their first summer.

Most weasels do not live to be more than a year old. Gamekeepers trap large numbers as vermin, and many are killed on the roads. Cats, owls, foxes and birds of prey will also kill weasels, but risk a hard fight in doing so.

Notes and Sketches

Long, pointed head

Rolls of flesh

SITES GUIDE

When grey seals spend a long time at sea, they rest and even sleep by 'bottling', holding themselves vertical in the water like a bottle with only their head showing so they can see, hear and breathe. You may see grey seals at most coastal sites, but especially at 1–3, 6, 8, 27, 28, 46–49, 55, 56 and 61.

Grey seal *Halichoerus grypus*

Grey (or Atlantic) seals may be seen off most of Britain's coasts but are most numerous around Scotland, particularly the offshore islands. They gather to breed on shore, sometimes in their hundreds, from September to December and are legally protected in the United Kingdom during these months. Outside the breeding season the seals spend much of their time at sea, sometimes for weeks on end, but haul themselves onto rocks or the shore to bask from time to time. While moulting, about March, the seals rest for long periods on rocks above high-tide level. Their bright coats show up newly moulted seals.

Fish are the seals' main food, adults eating a daily average of about 22 lb (10 kg), although they do not feed every day. In the last 50 years seal numbers have steadily increased. Colonies on places like the Farne Islands have become very overcrowded, causing damage to the soil and a lot of disease among pups. Because of their large numbers and their fish consumption, and also because they carry parasites that are transmitted to fish, there have been attempts at regular licensed culling (selective killing). These aroused so much public hostility that grey seals are now mostly left alone.

Commonest around rocky shores, mainly off north and west coasts of Britain.

When dry, a male seal's fur is a dark, blotched grey or brownish-grey. When wet it looks almost black. The head is long and pointed and the body very portly, with thick rolls of flesh folding around the neck. Male (bull) about 7 ft (2·1 m) long, female (cow) about 6 ft (1·8 m).

Notes and Sketches

Rounded head

Short muzzle

A common seal often basks with body arched so that its hind flippers and small, rounded head are raised. Seals vary in colour but are mottled with dark spots. From a distance they look pale when dry. Male 68 in. (173 cm) long, female smaller.

Mottled coat

SITES GUIDE

Common seals mate at sea and give birth in June or July on an exposed rock or sand bank. Their pups can swim straightaway and suckle on land or in the water. Look for the rounded heads of common seals at coastal sites around Ireland and in the east and north of Britain and particularly at sites 49, 52, 53 and 70.

May be seen off south coast but does not breed there. Rare off west of England, Wales.

In the water the seal's very rounded head looks like a buoy or fishing float. Its short muzzle and V-shaped nostrils help to distinguish it from a grey seal, which has nostrils that are almost parallel.

Common seal *Phoca vitulina*

Although common seals are often seen in groups of more than 100 basking contentedly in the sun, they are not really social animals. Unlike grey seals, they do not live in organised herds, nor are they noisy, even at breeding time. Common seals are placid, and tend to be found on sand-banks around sheltered shores such as estuaries and sea lochs.

Common seals will, however, haul themselves on to sea-weed-covered rocks close to deep water to bask, often returning to the same place day after day and departing to feed only when the incoming tide displaces them. On sand-banks they allow the outgoing tide to strand them on the highest point, a good lookout position where they may stay for several hours. If disturbed they move close to the water's edge, ready for a quick getaway. They have good eyesight, on land or underwater, and unless they are asleep it is not easy to approach them on open sand-banks. About 6,000 common seals, one-third of the British population, live around The Wash but they travel considerable distances along the east coast, probably following fish shoals. Common seals are protected by law during the breeding season (June 1 – August 31). They may live for 20–30 years.

Notes and Sketches

Most fallow deer are in full summer colouring by mid-June after a moult of about 40 days. The long, black, white-fringed tail and white, black-bordered rump are distinctive. The buck has broad-bladed (palmate) antlers and a prominent Adam's apple. Buck about 37 in. (95 cm) high at shoulder; doe slightly smaller.

Broad-bladed antlers

Typical summer coat

Long tail

Fallow deer *Dama dama*

Wild herds of fallow deer have lived for centuries in ancient forests such as the New Forest, Epping Forest and the Forest of Dean. They were a favourite quarry of medieval huntsmen, and later became the first choice for gracing the parks of hundreds of stately homes. During this century, animals that have escaped from parks have established many feral herds.

The fallow is unusual among deer because there are several colour varieties. Chestnut-brown with white spots is the typical summer colouring, but some animals, known as menil, are pale brown with spots, and there are intermediates between the two as well as both black and white varieties. Park herds may be all one colour but in the wild mixed herds are more usual.

Fallow deer may be seen feeding at any time, but dawn and dusk are generally favoured in the wild. By day they rest and ruminate in undergrowth or undisturbed pasture. Rutting time – the October to November mating period – is the most exciting time to watch them as the male (buck) herds together a group of females (does). Rival bucks fight fiercely, often with much clashing of antlers and furious charging until one retires hurt or defeated and the other takes the harem.

Most wild herds in south and east. Common in parks all over Britain.

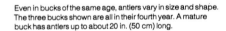

Even in bucks of the same age, antlers vary in size and shape. The three bucks shown are all in their fourth year. A mature buck has antlers up to about 20 in. (50 cm) long.

Notes and Sketches

Many-tined antlers

Buff rump

Britain's native red deer takes its name from the bright red-brown of its summer coat. It has a short tail, usually held close against its buff-coloured rump. Mature stags have antlers with many points (tines). Antlers can grow to about 28 in. (70 cm) long. Stag about 48 in. (120 cm) high at shoulder.

Biggest wild herds found in Scotland, Devon, New Forest, Cumbria. Common in parks.

SITES GUIDE

Red deer were originally woodland animals but as forests have disappeared they have adapted to living on moors and open hillsides. The stags have difficulty in obtaining sufficient calcium to grow their antlers each year and may gnaw the old antlers which they have shed. They may be seen at 7–9, 41, 42, 49, 51, 53, 54, 58, 59, 69.

Red deer *Cervus elaphus*

Scotland is the stronghold of Britain's wild red deer – the largest of our native animals. There are probably about a quarter of a million red deer in the Highlands and Islands. Most other wild herds are on Exmoor and in the Quantock Hills, the New Forest, Thetford Forest and the Lake District.

Except at rutting time in autumn, red deer stags (adult males) live in separate groups from the hinds (females). Deer in woodland live in small groups, sometimes resting and ruminating by day and emerging to graze at night. Highland deer are usually seen in larger herds, moving up the hillsides by day to feed on grasses, heather and lichens and sheltering in the deeper heather or woods at night. In summer they usually keep to the higher hill slopes, following the growth of new heather. In winter they move to lower ground. The red deer's bright summer coat changes to a thicker grey-brown from about September to May. Although Highland deer are hardy and can scrape through the snow to find food, many die in severe weather. Red deer are now being farmed for venison, mainly in Scotland. The deer are kept in a large enclosure and given hay and other foods to help them through winter.

Notes and Sketches

The hind is slightly smaller than the stag. In winter the coat is greyish-brown and the white rump prominent. Hock glands stand out as raised cushions on the hind legs.

White rump

Rounded ears

SITES GUIDE

If alarmed, the sika deer will first turn to face the source of danger before deciding whether or not to flee. If it does run away, it displays a very conspicuous white rump or caudal patch, which it flares to signal the danger to other deer. Sika deer may be seen at 6, 15, 53, 54, 69 and 70.

Distribution patchy. Herds in wild are all derived from escaped or released animals.

The sika deer is spotted in summer, with a bright chestnut-brown coat. Its ears are rounded, and lighter hair on the forehead darkens at the brow to give the deer a frowning look. It has a white tail, often with a dark stripe, and a white rump with dark edging. Stag 32 in. (80 cm) high at shoulder.

Sika deer *Cervus nippon*

Unlike its close relative the red deer, the sika deer is not native to Britain but was introduced about 120 years ago to a number of deer parks. It originates from parts of eastern Asia, including the USSR, China and Japan, where it is known as the spotted deer. Feral herds in various parts of Britain are derived from escaped or released animals. One of the most flourishing populations is in Dorset, the descendants of deer introduced to Brownsea Island in 1896, some of which swam across Poole Harbour to the mainland. Because of their close relationship, sika and red deer will interbreed and produce fertile hybrid offspring. It is feared that where the two live in the same area, such interbreeding could destroy the purity of the native red deer as a species.

Sika deer are most active at dawn and dusk, when they leave the cover of the undergrowth to graze. Rutting takes place from late September to early November. Mature males (stags) mark out their territories by thrashing bushes and fraying tree bark with their antlers, and fight off rivals to gather a harem of females (hinds). A sika stag's call at rutting time is quite distinctive – a loud whistle repeated several times. Other rutting calls range from a 'raspberry' to a roar.

Notes and Sketches

Black nose

White chin
patch

Buff
rump

A forest deer spreading in
many areas, especially to new
plantations.

A roe deer's summer coat is a sleek, foxy red
with a buff patch on the rump. Its white chin
patch and black nose, sometimes with a white
rim or patch above, are distinctive. The ears
are large and furry inside. A buck's antlers are
roughened (pearled) near the base. About
25 in. (64 cm) high at the top of the shoulder.

Antlers are cast in
November or December.
During winter new ones
grow, protected from frost
by a woolly skin (velvet)
rubbed off by May.

Sites Guide

Roe deer spend the day lying
up in cover, sometimes in
woodland, sometimes in a
tiny patch of scrub. They will
scrape an area clear of dead
leaves and lie on the soil of
the woodland floor. Such
scrapes are readily identified
by the wiry and crimped
white hairs that roe deer
leave behind. Look out for
them at 5, 8, 12, 13, 15, 16,
19–22, 40–45, 47, 48, 50–
54.

Roe deer *Capreolus capreolus*

In the Middle Ages the roe deer, the smallest of our native deer,
was widespread in Britain. Later it gradually disappeared, no
one is sure why, surviving in only a few places. About 100 years
ago the deer was re-introduced to parts of England and has
spread to many woodland and upland areas.

Roe deer generally keep to cover, and are usually seen in
small groups or singly. They are most active at dawn and dusk
and feed mainly on tree shoots or shrubs. Rutting, or mating,
takes place in July and August. A male (buck) establishes his
territory at the end of May, when his antlers are hard and fully
grown. He rubs against trees and bushes to scent them and barks
at rival bucks and chases them off, sometimes fighting. Females
(does) entering the territory are courted and mated, yearling
does being ready for mating before older does. Roe deer are the
only hoofed mammals in which implantation of the fertilised
egg is delayed. It does not occur until December and the young
are born in the following May or June. Twins are common and
there are sometimes triplets. New-born young (kids) seen lying
among bracken, brambles or grass should not be disturbed. The
doe is near by and returns to suckle them several times a day.

Notes and Sketches

Rounded back

Short antlers

The smallest British deer, the muntjac has a glossy, red-brown summer coat and is distinguished by its rather rounded back. There is some white round the edge of the tail, but the amount varies. The buck has short antlers and prominent fang-like teeth in his upper jaw. Buck about 19 in. (48 cm) high at top of shoulder; doe slightly smaller.

Found in woodland and scrub. Introduced to Bedfordshire, Hertfordshire; is spreading.

Muntjac *Muntiacus reevesi*

Although it is called the barking deer in its native Asia, the muntjac is not the only barking deer in Britain, for several other species also bark. The Chinese, or Reeves's, muntjac was introduced to the Duke of Bedford's Woburn estate in Bedfordshire about 1900. Since then the descendants of escaped or released animals have become well established in England, and are still spreading. Their increase is no doubt due to the fact that females (does) can conceive a few days after fawning and may give birth every seven months. Unlike native British deer, they have no fixed breeding season.

Muntjac are active by day or night but are most often seen at dusk, feeding on grass, brambles and other plants, including ivy and yew. Their winter coats are duller and thicker than their summer coats. In common with all deer, muntjac have scent glands with secretions that are probably a means of communication. They include forehead glands. To mark territory they rub their heads against the ground or a tree to leave scent. A male (buck) establishes a territory that includes the home area of several does and will fight rival bucks. He uses his fine-pointed fang-like teeth as weapons rather than his antlers.

Notes and Sketches

Spreading horns

Shaggy coat

SITES GUIDE

Goats are sure-footed, agile creatures which climb steep rocky cliffs very easily, often using this skill as a means of escape. They are both grazers and browsers and can do considerable damage to trees and shrubs if other food is scarce. They may be seen at 6, 53, 54, 66.

Isolated herds in rocky areas of the north and west. Small herds on some islands.

The small, shaggy feral goat is a free-living descendant of domestic goats of the past, before modern breeds were developed. Both sexes have horns, which may sweep back or, more often, spread outwards. Male 30 in. (76 cm) high at shoulder. Female smaller.

Feral goat *Capra* (domestic)

Stone Age farmers first brought goats to Britain, and there have been herds of feral goats – descendants of domestic animals gone wild – in mountainous areas for well over 1,000 years. Two-hundred years ago, shaggy feral goats were commoner than sheep in many places, but today the remaining herds are small and isolated. There is considerable variation in colour and size between individuals, as with many feral species once the rigours of selective breeding have been removed. Because isolation prevents interbreeding, the goats in one place tend to be different from those in another.

For most of the year the goats keep to high, rocky mountainsides or cliff tops, in winter descending to grassy valleys or the neighbourhood of farms in search of food. Towards the end of winter the herds disperse and females go off to give birth to kids. At first a kid stays hidden among boulders, visited by its mother two or three times a day. When about ten days old a kid is strong enough to follow its mother, and by summer females and youngsters have gathered into a herd. Kids are too big for most predators, but many die of exposure. Adults are better able to withstand damp and drizzle, and often live for five years.

Notes and Sketches

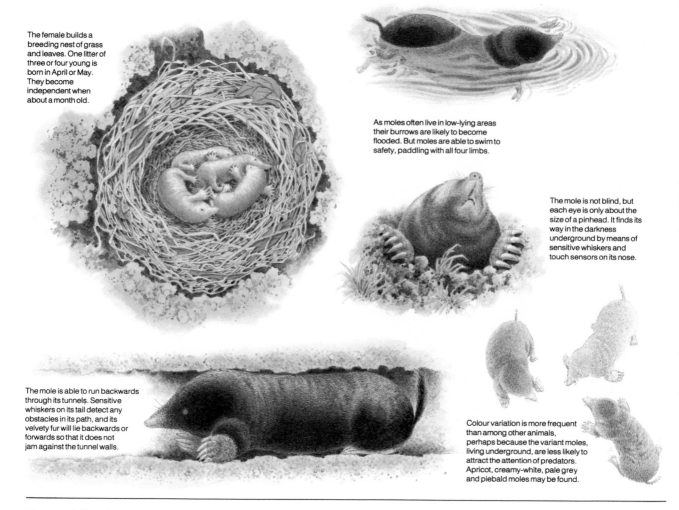

The female builds a breeding nest of grass and leaves. One litter of three or four young is born in April or May. They become independent when about a month old.

As moles often live in low-lying areas their burrows are likely to become flooded. But moles are able to swim to safety, paddling with all four limbs.

The mole is not blind, but each eye is only about the size of a pinhead. It finds its way in the darkness underground by means of sensitive whiskers and touch sensors on its nose.

The mole is able to run backwards through its tunnels. Sensitive whiskers on its tail detect any obstacles in its path, and its velvety fur will lie backwards or forwards so that it does not jam against the tunnel walls.

Colour variation is more frequent than among other animals, perhaps because the variant moles, living underground, are less likely to attract the attention of predators. Apricot, creamy-white, pale grey and piebald moles may be found.

Notes and Sketches

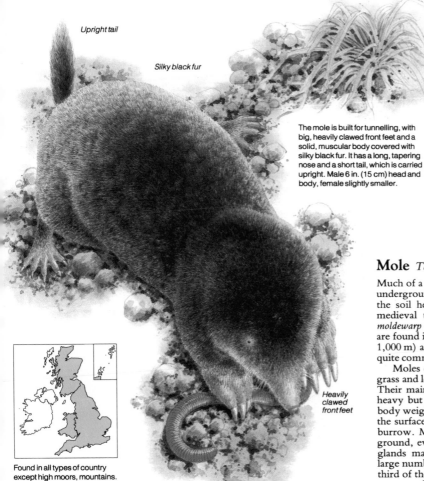

Upright tail

Silky black fur

The mole is built for tunnelling, with big, heavily clawed front feet and a solid, muscular body covered with silky black fur. It has a long, tapering nose and a short tail, which is carried upright. Male 6 in. (15 cm) head and body, female slightly smaller.

Heavily clawed front feet

Found in all types of country except high moors, mountains. Lives mostly underground.

SITES GUIDE

Moles leave one of the most obvious animal signs in the countryside, the molehill. In areas with shallow soils, you can sometimes see where the mole has been unable to dig downwards and has pushed along almost at the surface leaving a ridge in the ground. Moles are very common in Britain and may be seen at most of the sites in this book. They do not occur in Ireland.

Mole *Talpa europaea*

Much of a mole's life is spent in a burrow system that it tunnels underground, so it is not often seen. Its presence is evident from the soil heaps (molehills) it makes while tunnelling, and in medieval times one of the names given to the mole was *moldewarp* (earth thrower). Active throughout the year, moles are found in most places except ground above 3,000 ft (roughly 1,000 m) and in very acid soils. In woodlands, where they are quite common, molehills are often hidden by leaves.

Moles come to the surface to collect nesting material – dry grass and leaves – and also to look for food when the soil is dry. Their main food is earthworms, which, being full of soil, are heavy but not very nutritious, so moles eat at least half their body weight in food every day. Young moles probably come to the surface to find new homes when they leave their mother's burrow. Moles are most vulnerable to predators when above ground, even though they emerge mainly at night. Their skin glands make them distasteful to carnivorous mammals, but large numbers are eaten by tawny owls and barn owls. About a third of the mole population survives for more than a year, but not many live to be three years old.

Notes and Sketches

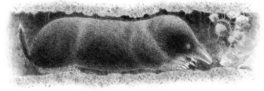

A mole regularly patrols its tunnels to eat whatever soil animals – such as worms, beetle larvae and slugs – have fallen from the walls. Tunnels are longest and molehills most numerous in poor soil, where the mole's food supply is sparse.

Although it can travel backwards in its tunnel, a mole can also turn in the opposite direction by doing a forward roll.

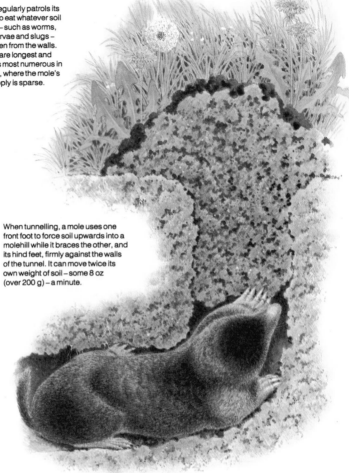

When tunnelling, a mole uses one front foot to force soil upwards into a molehill while it braces the other, and its hind feet, firmly against the walls of the tunnel. It can move twice its own weight of soil – some 8 oz (over 200 g) – a minute.

How moles live and feed underground

Because of their digging activities, moles are considered a nuisance by many gardeners and farmers. Most tunnels are quite near the surface, and tunnelling may interfere with the roots of garden plants and crops. Occasionally tunnels are so near the surface that the soil is forced up in a long ridge – once these were thought (wrongly) to be 'love runs' made by male moles seeking a mate. Molehills each contain about 2 lb (1 kg) of soil. They disfigure lawns and in fields are an inconvenience to farm machinery such as combine harvesters; they may even damage them. But moles can also be quite useful. They eat a lot of insect larvae that are damaging to grass and root crops, and their tunnelling helps to aerate the soil – important in peaty and waterlogged areas.

In days gone by, country parishes often employed a professional mole-catcher to trap and dig up moles in places where they were not wanted. In one season, a mole-catcher might catch 1,000 moles and earn a small income by selling the skins for hat and coat trimmings. As late as the 1950s about a million moles were being trapped every year in Britain. Since synthetic furs became common, however, catching moles for their skins has become no longer worth the effort.

Notes and Sketches

Each mole has its own burrow, a system of firm-walled tunnels about 2 in. (50 mm) wide and 1½ in. (40 mm) high which may be about 200 yds (roughly 200 m) long.

Molehills are heaps of displaced soil pushed to the surface up vertical tunnels at intervals while a mole is burrowing. They are not burrow entrances. Molehill soil is loose and fresh, unlike an anthill, which is steep-sided and grassy.

Anthill

Fortress

A mole does spend some of its time on the surface, especially at night. This is when it is most likely to be caught by a predator such as an owl.

Long soil ridge

The breeding nest is the size of a football. It usually has several exits. An extra large molehill, or fortress, may cover the nest chamber in early spring.

The mole is very aggressive and normally chases an intruding mole from its burrow, except briefly for mating in late February or March.

Notes and Sketches

From three to five young are born, usually in June or July, in a nest of leaves and grass. The young are blind and pink at first, but sprout a few white, bristly spines within hours of birth.

An adult hedgehog has some 5,000 spines on its back. When it rolls into a ball, its spiky coat protects it from all but the most determined predators. The young, which have fewer spines and weaker rolling-up muscles, are more vulnerable.

During the first two weeks of life, young hedgehogs grow more and more brown spines alongside the white spines. Their eyes open at about 14 days old. By the time they are from five to six weeks old, they have more than 2,000 spines.

Spines are modified hairs that can be raised for defence. They are about 1 in. (25 mm) long and very sharp. Each spine lasts for a year or more before it drops out and a replacement is grown.

Notes and Sketches

Spiny coat

Hairy face

Widespread on farmland and in urban areas. Scarce on moors, in conifer forests.

Unmistakable because of its spiny coat, a hedgehog also has long, coarse hair on its face and underparts. It is active mostly at night, but young or sickly animals may be seen by day. It relies mainly on smell to find food. About 10 in. (25 cm) long.

Hedgehog *Erinaceus europaeus*

Britain's only spiny mammal, the hedgehog has been a familiar creature of gardens, hedgerows and meadows for centuries. It features in some curious folk tales. They tell of hedgehogs picking up fruit on their spines and of hedgehogs sucking milk from cows, but such behaviour is improbable.

Beetles, caterpillars and earthworms make up most of the hedgehog's diet, but it will also eat birds' eggs, slugs, snails and carrion. In winter, when such foods are in short supply, the hedgehog hibernates in a sheltered nest of leaves and grass and lives off reserves of body fat built up in the autumn. Hedgehogs are ready to breed in April, soon after hibernation ends. Most young are born in early summer, but late litters in September are common, especially if the first litter has been lost. Late-born young often do not survive the winter. A mother disturbed in her nest may eat or abandon new-born young, but will carry older ones by the scruff of the neck to a safer place. Youngsters start to take solid food at about a month old, and at night the mother leads her family out in procession to forage. The young become independent at about six weeks old. The male takes no part in rearing them, and may not even live near by.

Notes and Sketches

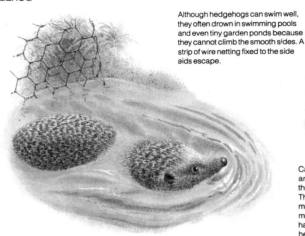

Although hedgehogs can swim well, they often drown in swimming pools and even tiny garden ponds because they cannot climb the smooth sides. A strip of wire netting fixed to the side aids escape.

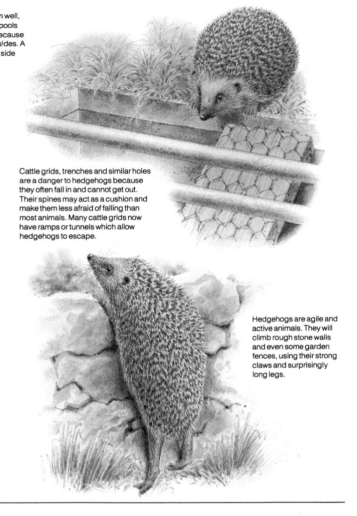

Cattle grids, trenches and similar holes are a danger to hedgehogs because they often fall in and cannot get out. Their spines may act as a cushion and make them less afraid of falling than most animals. Many cattle grids now have ramps or tunnels which allow hedgehogs to escape.

Helping hedgehogs to survive

Although few animals prey on them, hedgehogs face many hazards to survival. Every year thousands are killed by motor vehicles because they react to danger by rolling up. There is little evidence to support the theory that more are tending to run from danger, nor would running necessarily save their lives, although they can run quite fast. As hedgehogs feed on garden pests, it is in a gardener's interest to encourage them. Accidents that befall some hedgehogs in gardens are drowning in ponds or becoming entangled in netting. The use of garden chemicals such as insecticides and possibly slug pellets is also a threat to hedgehog survival. Many such chemicals are present in minute quantities in beetles and caterpillars, and as hedgehogs eat hundreds of them every month they can soon accumulate enough poison to damage their health.

Hedgehogs face their greatest risks during hibernation. They may die of cold or be disturbed by fire or flood, or someone may wreck their nest. Gardeners can help by leaving piles of fallen leaves undisturbed behind sheds and under hedges. More than half of all hedgehogs do not survive their first winter. The remainder may live two or three years, rarely five or six.

Hedgehogs are agile and active animals. They will climb rough stone walls and even some garden fences, using their strong claws and surprisingly long legs.

Notes and Sketches

Extra food such as a bowl of bread and milk helps garden hedgehogs to fatten up for winter hibernation. They will go more than ½ mile (about 0·5 km) for such a treat. A hedgehog will die during winter if its reserves of body fat are inadequate.

If a hedgehog is seen to froth at the mouth and twist itself about, it is not sick but is spreading the frothy saliva on its fur and spines with its tongue. The purpose of this behaviour is unknown, but it is quite normal.

Hedgehogs sniff through garden litter to nose out woodlice and slugs. Eating poisoned creatures can lead to a hedgehog's death. Use garden chemicals sparingly.

Notes and Sketches

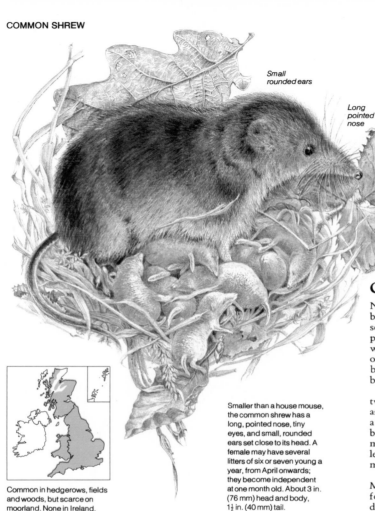

Small rounded ears

Long pointed nose

SITES GUIDE

This is one of the most frequently seen small mammals, but only after it has died. The glands under the shrew's skin make it distasteful to many predators and so its corpse is usually dropped, often by a path where it is noticed by passers by. Listen for, as well as look for, common shrews at 11, 15, 21, 27, 29–33, 35–38, 41, 43, 47–51, 53.

Smaller than a house mouse, the common shrew has a long, pointed nose, tiny eyes, and small, rounded ears set close to its head. A female may have several litters of six or seven young a year, from April onwards; they become independent at one month old. About 3 in. (76 mm) head and body, 1½ in. (40 mm) tail.

Common in hedgerows, fields and woods, but scarce on moorland. None in Ireland.

Common shrew *Sorex araneus*

No common shrew can tolerate another in its territory, except briefly at breeding time. When two common shrews meet, both scream at each other with shrill, aggressive squeaks, which is perhaps why the term 'shrewish' is applied to a scolding woman. The squeaking can be heard for some distance and is often the only sign that shrews are near by. They are rarely seen because they spend three-quarters of their time underground, but are probably one of Britain's most abundant mammals.

Active by day or night, the shrew is constantly on the move, twittering and muttering and poking its long nose here and there as it scurries along in search of food such as woodlice. It snatches a brief rest every hour or two, but expends so much energy in its bustling life that it will starve to death if it goes without food for more than about three hours. The shrew forages in the soil or leaf litter, along tiny tunnels it digs itself or which have been made by small rodents.

Common shrews may live to be a year old – few live longer. Many fall prey to owls, other predators being deterred by the foul-tasting glands in the shrew's skin, which also give it a distinctive odour. Cats may kill shrews, but rarely eat them.

Notes and Sketches

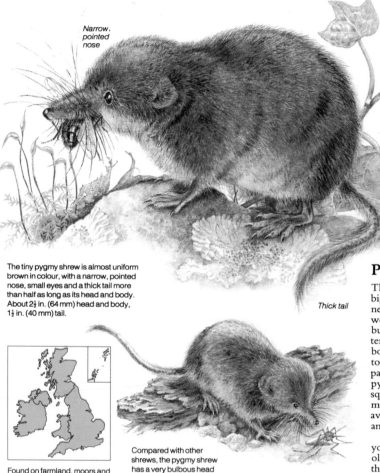

Narrow, pointed nose

Thick tail

The tiny pygmy shrew is almost uniform brown in colour, with a narrow, pointed nose, small eyes and a thick tail more than half as long as its head and body. About 2½ in. (64 mm) head and body, 1½ in. (40 mm) tail.

Found on farmland, moors and in forests. Widespread, but scarcer than common shrew.

Compared with other shrews, the pygmy shrew has a very bulbous head and a short, narrow snout.

Pygmy shrew *Sorex minutus*

The pygmy shrew is Britain's smallest mammal, not much bigger than a stag beetle or longhorn beetle. It is so tiny that it is near the limit at which a warm-blooded animal can exist – if it were any smaller its body surface would be too extensive for its bulk and it would lose heat too rapidly to maintain a warm body temperature. The shrew does in fact lose so much energy as body heat that it must constantly search for food, and will starve to death if it fails to eat for more than two hours. Hardly ever pausing for more than a few minutes in its busy foraging, the pygmy shrew may explore more than 1,500 sq. yds (about 1,250 sq. m) of territory regularly. It bustles along shallow tunnels made by other animals in the soil, leaf litter or vegetation, and avidly consumes small soil creatures such as spiders, tiny beetles and insect larvae.

Females give birth to several litters each summer. The youngsters grow quickly and leave the nest at about three weeks old. Those born in early summer may be raising families themselves within a few weeks. But many shrews die within a few months of birth, and those that survive to breed the following year do not live through a second winter.

Notes and Sketches

Black coat

White eyebrows
and ear tips

Found in farmland, woods and
hedgerows. Widespread, but
may be scarce in some areas.

The water shrew's black coat and
silvery-white underparts meet in a
sharp line along its flanks, and its
eyebrows and ear tips are often white.
Juveniles have duller coats than
adults. About 3⅜ in. (86 mm) head and
body, 2¼ in. (55 mm) tail.

Water shrew *Neomys fodiens*

All shrews tend to be more abundant in damp places, where
their prey is common – worms, insect larvae and small spiders,
for example. Water shrews will also take to the water to hunt in
ponds and streams for other prey such as fish, tadpoles and even
quite large frogs. However, they also often live away from the
water, even on dry downland, and some inhabit stony beaches
where they probably feed on sandhoppers and flies along the
high-tide line. Active by day or night, the shrews eat roughly
their own weight in food daily.

Except for females raising families, water shrews normally
live alone in shallow burrow systems they dig themselves.
Sometimes a burrow is in a bank and has an underwater
entrance. Two or three litters containing from three to eight
young may be born in a year, from May onwards. Some females
have their first litter when only two or three months old, but
most do not breed until the summer following their birth.
Although they may live for up to 18 months, water shrews
mostly die young or are taken by predators such as owls, pike
and mink. Numbers tend to fluctuate, the shrews apparently
disappearing from an area then reappearing after several years.

Notes and Sketches

Small, finely haired ears

Thick, scaly tail

Common around buildings, in farms and hedgerows. Less usual on high ground, moors.

The brown (or common) rat will eat anything and thrives where there are food stores or waste. It has coarse, grey-brown fur, small finely haired ears and a thick, scaly tail always shorter than its head and body. Male up to 11 in. (28 cm) head and body, 9 in. (23 cm) tail. Female smaller.

SITES GUIDE

This rat has gained a bad reputation as a result of its successful lifestyle. It rapidly found a niche alongside humans and it has taken full advantage of the abundant food supply to multiply as quickly as possible. Brown rats often take to water and may be seen most easily in streams or rivers. They have been recorded at 15, 25, 29, 31, 33, 38, 48, 49, 53, 56.

Brown rat *Rattus norvegicus*

A widespread pest, the brown rat fouls food stores and gnaws stored goods. It spread to Britain in the early 18th century, probably from Russia, and is found not only in buildings but also in many places out of doors, such as rubbish tips and muddy shores where debris is washed up by the tide. Very large populations often build up in farms, where there is plenty of food even though combine harvesters have done away with the corn ricks that once harboured thousands of rats. In a fine summer, young rats may spread into hedgerows and lay-bys far from buildings. Brown rats are also at home in sewers, where they are especially liable to pick up and transmit diseases.

Where food and shelter are abundant, a female brown rat can produce five litters a year totalling 50 young, all able to breed at three months old. But many young rats are caught by cats, owls, foxes and other predators. Rat numbers are also controlled by the use of special poisons that prevent blood from clotting – although some rats have developed a resistance to them in the past ten years. The white rats of pet shops and laboratories are a specially bred form of brown rat. Unlike their aggressive wild cousins, they are tame, inoffensive and do not smell.

Notes and Sketches

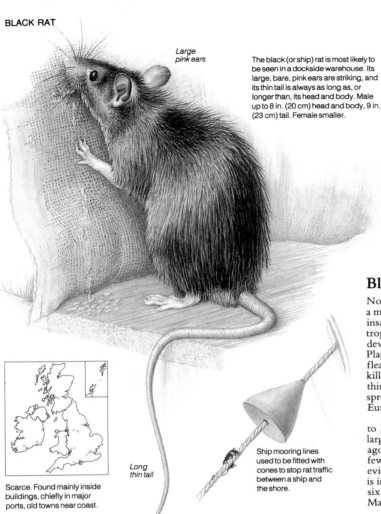

Large pink ears

The black (or ship) rat is most likely to be seen in a dockside warehouse. Its large, bare, pink ears are striking, and its thin tail is always as long as, or longer than, its head and body. Male up to 8 in. (20 cm) head and body, 9 in. (23 cm) tail. Female smaller.

Long thin tail

Scarce. Found mainly inside buildings, chiefly in major ports, old towns near coast.

Ship mooring lines used to be fitted with cones to stop rat traffic between a ship and the shore.

Sites Guide

Black rats are extremely agile climbers and can scramble up ropes and wires with ease. Like brown rats, they have a greasy coat which leaves stains on routes that they use frequently. Strangely, the black rat – otherwise known as the ship's rat – hates entering water. Black rats are now rare in Britain and have only been recorded at 15.

Black rat *Rattus rattus*

Notorious for its role in carrying plague, the black rat thrives in a man-made environment, and was numerous in the untidy and insanitary towns of medieval Europe. The rat originated in tropical Asia, but spread to Europe as trade between countries developed; it reached Britain probably in the 11th century. Plague was rife in Asia, the virus being transmitted by the rat flea. During the 14th century, a massive outbreak of disease killed some 25 million people in Europe, including more than a third of Britain's population, and was thought to be plague, spread by the rat flea. But modern research suggests that the European killer disease may not have been plague after all.

Because of its tropical origins, in Britain the black rat prefers to live in warm, sheltered buildings. Since the coming of the larger, more aggressive and adaptable brown rat some 200 years ago, the black rat has disappeared from most of its old haunts. A few open-air colonies exist on islands such as Lundy, the rats evidently feeding mainly on plants, but their long-term survival is in doubt. Black rats usually have from three to five litters of six or seven young a year; they mature at about four months old. Man and domestic cats are their chief enemies.

Notes and Sketches

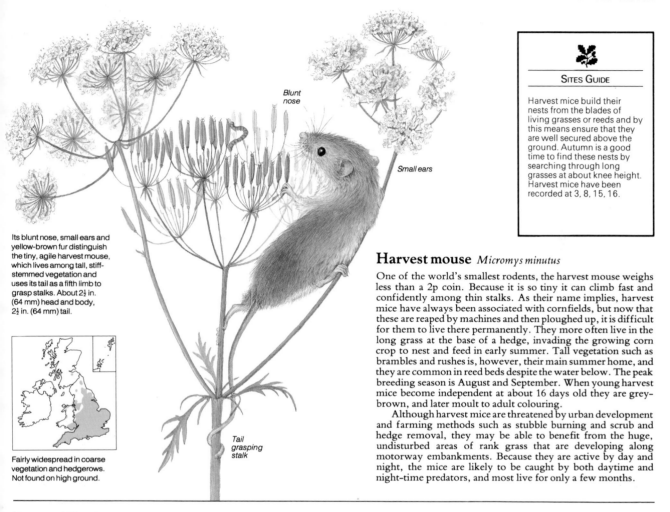

Blunt nose

Small ears

Its blunt nose, small ears and yellow-brown fur distinguish the tiny, agile harvest mouse, which lives among tall, stiff-stemmed vegetation and uses its tail as a fifth limb to grasp stalks. About 2½ in. (64 mm) head and body, 2½ in. (64 mm) tail.

Fairly widespread in coarse vegetation and hedgerows. Not found on high ground.

Tail grasping stalk

Harvest mouse *Micromys minutus*

One of the world's smallest rodents, the harvest mouse weighs less than a 2p coin. Because it is so tiny it can climb fast and confidently among thin stalks. As their name implies, harvest mice have always been associated with cornfields, but now that these are reaped by machines and then ploughed up, it is difficult for them to live there permanently. They more often live in the long grass at the base of a hedge, invading the growing corn crop to nest and feed in early summer. Tall vegetation such as brambles and rushes is, however, their main summer home, and they are common in reed beds despite the water below. The peak breeding season is August and September. When young harvest mice become independent at about 16 days old they are grey-brown, and later moult to adult colouring.

Although harvest mice are threatened by urban development and farming methods such as stubble burning and scrub and hedge removal, they may be able to benefit from the huge, undisturbed areas of rank grass that are developing along motorway embankments. Because they are active by day and night, the mice are likely to be caught by both daytime and night-time predators, and most live for only a few months.

Notes and Sketches

Pointed nose

Greasy fur

Scaly tail

Many kinds of stored food will attract the house mouse, which is mostly active at night. Alert and nimble, it has prominent ears, big eyes and a pointed face. Its grey-brown coat is greasy and glistening and its tail long and scaly. Unlike other mice, it is smelly. About 3¼ in. (83 mm) head and body, 3¼ in. (83 mm) tail.

SITES GUIDE

These adaptable rodents exploit every opportunity to obtain food. Some have even taken to living in cold stores, growing longer warmer coats in order to do so. House mice can be found throughout the British Isles and Ireland and may be seen at all the sites.

Widespread, mostly in and around buildings, but also in hedgerows and on farmland.

Mice gnaw to wear down their chisel-like front teeth, which are growing all the time. They can cause fires by gnawing through insulation on electric wires, and are sometimes electrocuted.

House mouse *Mus musculus*

Unlike other mice, the house mouse has a strong smell and greasy fur. It taints the places it lives in – homes, warehouses, hospitals and other public buildings. Mice also leave their black droppings and their urine about, carry diseases and parasites, and cause damage by their gnawing. Although house mice live for only about 18 months, and many die in their first winter, it is hard for the humans they live with to get rid of them. They breed so fast that in one summer the mice from one nest will have multiplied many times over. Females bear from five to ten litters a year with five or six young in a litter. The young leave the nest at three weeks old and three weeks later the females among them are ready to breed.

House mice live within a yard or two of their food supply and move on only when food is short. They are easily transported accidentally among food or goods and, with the spread of humans, have colonised most of the earth from their first home in Asia. The species essentially lives with man, indoors. When the Scottish islands of St Kilda were deserted in 1930, the house mouse – probably a resident since Viking times – became extinct within a few years.

Notes and Sketches

Large ears

Yellow streak

Long tail

Its sandy-brown coat and large ears and eyes help to distinguish the wood mouse. The underparts are white, with a yellow streak on the chest, and the tail is lightly haired. About 3¾ in. (95 mm) head and body, tail longer.

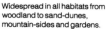

Widespread in all habitats from woodland to sand-dunes, mountain-sides and gardens.

When mice are frightened, they often wash and groom themselves. They sit on their haunches and lick vigorously at their armpits, forelimbs and belly.

Wood mouse *Apodemus sylvaticus*

Probably the most widespread and abundant British mammal, the wood mouse – also known as the long-tailed field mouse – is not confined to woodlands. It thrives equally well in more open places, even on moorlands and mountain-sides, and is also common in gardens, where it often lives near sheds and out-buildings and causes people to think house mice have moved in. However, unlike house mice, wood mice do not smell strongly.

The wood mouse is very active, running and bounding from place to place and venturing into open places where other small mammals will rarely go. Although it moves only under cover of darkness, it is frequently taken by predators, especially owls and cats. Most wood mice stay in the same general area but may travel a quarter of a mile (400 m) in one night. In winter they sometimes go into a torpid state – almost like hibernation – in which they use far less energy than usual. This helps them survive food shortages. The population is at its lowest at the end of winter, but numbers soon build up. Breeding starts in March, and a female may bear four litters, each of about five young, in a year. Wood mice are generally short-lived; the maximum life-span in the wild is rarely more than two years.

Notes and Sketches

Yellow
collar

Orange-
brown
flank

Found in woods, hedgerows,
but distribution is patchy.
Much rarer than wood mouse.

The yellow-necked mouse looks very
much like the wood mouse, but is
distinguished by its distinct yellow
collar. It is also bigger and heavier
than the wood mouse, and its sandy-
brown coat has more orange on the
flanks. About 4 in. (10 cm) head and
body, tail usually longer.

Sites Guide

This is a surprisingly arboreal
rodent whose forays take it
high into the canopies of
trees in search of buds in the
spring or fruits and seeds in
the autumn. It is also known
to nest well above the
ground, sometimes in boxes
erected for dormice. Yellow-
necked mice have a limited
range in England and Wales
and may be seen at 11, 21,
23, 26.

Yellow-necked mouse *Apodemus flavicollis*

Not only does the yellow-necked mouse resemble a large,
sandy-coloured wood mouse, but it is very like the wood mouse
in its behaviour. Both mice are strictly nocturnal, with the big
ears and eyes of creatures that need to pick up in the dark the faint
sound or slight movement that warns of approaching danger,
and both climb well and often search for food among high
branches. Both are also found in woods, hedgerows and gardens. This seems to contradict a basic biological principle that no
two animals can live in the same place and share the same food
supply without one ultimately displacing the other. The yellow-
necked mouse might be expected to become dominant as it is
larger, but it is the wood mouse that occurs over most of Britain.
Yellow-necked mice occur only in the south, and even there
huge tracts of suitable woodland are apparently without them.
Where they do occur, yellow-necked mice may increase to
considerable numbers and then inexplicably disappear a year or
two later.

In parts of the south-east, where yellow-necked mice can be
quite common, they often go into gardens and even houses in
autumn – perhaps seeking a dry, sheltered place for the winter.

Notes and Sketches

Chubby face

Long, glossy fur

Although the water vole is about the same size as a brown rat, it differs in having a chubby face with a blunt nose, short furry ears almost hidden by its long, glossy, dark chocolate-brown fur, and a shorter tail. Male 8 in. (20 cm) head and body, 4¾ in. (12 cm) tail. Female slightly smaller.

Common in lowland Britain, but not in Ireland. Found by ponds, slow-running rivers.

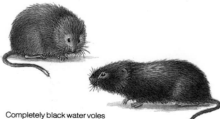

Completely black water voles occur, especially in Scotland. Voles with a white tail-tip are also more frequent in Scotland.

Water vole *Arvicola terrestris*

Water voles are often called water rats, but are only distantly related to rats. Brown rats do, like the voles, sometimes live in waterside burrows and may be seen swimming, but are rarely found far from buildings and often live in polluted water. Water voles prefer clean water in relatively undisturbed areas by lowland river banks or the fringes of ponds and lakes.

The harmless water vole feeds almost entirely on waterside plants, and spends most of its life in a narrow strip of land at the water's edge. Small heaps of droppings mark the limits of its home range. A male occupies about 140 yds (130 m) of bank, and often stays in the same area a long time, sometimes all its life. A female occupies only half the range of a male and will sometimes leave her regular haunts to live elsewhere. Young voles, which are very dark brown with a long, almost black, tail, are sometimes found away from water in damp woodland and grassy areas; they may be mistaken for field voles, although bigger and darker. Movement from a population often occurs when numbers are high after a good breeding season, or when shallow ponds are drying up because of dry weather. A water vole's normal life-span is 12–18 months.

Notes and Sketches

Hazelnuts are frequently eaten: The sharp-toothed bank vole gnaws a hole in the shell and takes out the kernel in small pieces.

Seeds, berries, nuts, fruit, green plants and fungi are all part of the bank vole's diet. Food may be stored underground or taken there to eat in safety.

Where there is sufficient thick undergrowth, the bank vole forages busily by day or night along a network of tunnels beaten through vegetation or dug underground.

Skomer vole

The Skomer vole found on Skomer Island, Dyfed, is twice as heavy as mainland voles and about 4¼ in. (11·5 cm) long in head and body. It is one of four larger island sub-species; the others are on Jersey, Mull and Raasay.

There may be four or five litters, each with four or five babies, between April and September. The nest is sometimes above ground, perhaps in a tree crevice, but often up to 4 in. (10 cm) below ground in a chamber reached by tunnels.

Notes and Sketches

Small ears

Blunt nose

Short tail

The bank vole can be distinguished from a mouse by its chubby appearance, blunt nose, small eyes and ears and short, furry tail. Adults have a glossy, chestnut-brown coat that may shade to grey on the belly. About 3½ in. (90 mm) head and body, up to 2⅜ in. (60 mm) tail.

Commonest in lowlands. Found in woods, hedges and scrub. Very limited in Ireland.

The bank vole has a redder coat and more prominent ears than a field vole. Young bank voles are grey-brown and more difficult to tell from field voles.

SITES GUIDE

Bank voles are better climbers than field voles and are quite at home scrambling around in hedges and even up in trees. They enjoy the fleshy parts of fruits such as haws and hips, and either eat these in the bush or take them underground to store and eat safely. Look out for voles at 3, 4, 14, 16, 18, 21, 27, 29, 31, 33, 37, 38, 40, 42, 43, 47, 48, 51–53, 69.

Bank vole *Clethrionomys glareolus*

After the wood mouse the bank vole is probably the most abundant of Britain's small rodents. It is more likely to be seen during daylight than the wood mouse, and tends to run and scurry rather than move in leaps and bounds. Although it may sometimes be found in long grass, wet places or on mountainsides, the bank vole much prefers to live where there is dense cover. It is rarely found far from bramble thickets, hedgerows and other woody scrub, and is common in country gardens. Each bank vole occupies a home range, and does not normally venture more than about 55 yds (50 m) from its nest. Males generally range more widely than females.

In mild years when there is plenty of food available, bank voles may begin breeding early and continue well into late autumn. A vole born early in the year may itself be raising a family within a few weeks, so the population builds up quickly. But fewer than half of those born survive the first few months. After they leave the nest at about 18 days old, young voles are often taken by predators such as weasels, or may die during cold, wet weather. The more robust survivors may live for 18 months. Bank voles have been found in Ireland only since 1964.

Notes and Sketches

Yellowy-brown fur

Short tail

Its yellow-brown colouring helps to distinguish the field vole from the red-brown bank vole. It is chubby like the bank vole, with a blunt nose and short ears, but it has a shorter, pinker tail and is also known as the short-tailed vole. About 4 in. (10 cm) head and body, 1½ in. (40 mm) tail.

Widespread in grassland and hedgerows in both lowlands and uplands. None in Ireland.

Adults are very belligerent. They compete for territory and are quick to fight in its defence.

SITES GUIDE

The field vole is often too timid to emerge to feed properly. Instead it will merely stick its head out of its hole and nibble the grass which is within reach. In a short time, the grasses immediately around the entrance are grazed short like a lawn. Look for signs of field voles at 4, 16, 21, 27, 28, 30–33, 35–38, 43, 48–53.

Field vole *Microtus agrestis*

Overgrown fields and places with long, rough grass are typically the home of the aptly named field vole, which particularly likes damp, tussocky grass. Aggressive and noisy, field voles utter loud squeaks and angry chattering noises as they defend their small territories, driving out other voles. Each vole makes runways among the grass stems, usually centred on the tussock where it nests; it feeds frequently, by day or night.

Field voles are taken by a host of predators, but are prolific breeders. Populations in a favourable habitat often increase rapidly to number in their thousands – a vole plague. The plague is followed by a rapid decline, probably due to less successful breeding because of overcrowding and heightened aggression. These high and low populations occur at intervals of from three to five years, often accompanied by similar fluctuations in predator populations. Field voles are very abundant for a few years in young forestry plantations, but as the trees grow they cast a dense shade and the grass dies, forcing the voles to go elsewhere. Some survive on the grassy fringes, from where they can quickly recolonise grassy areas that develop once trees are felled. The normal life–span is about a year.

Notes and Sketches

Bushy tail

Ear-tufts

Chestnut fur

The squirrel's ear-tufts are especially long in the winter (particularly on an adult), and give it a perky appearance.

Declining; mostly gone from south. Mainly restricted to large areas of mature forest.

The long, silky winter coat is chocolate brown, the fur on the back sometimes looking dark grey. The tail is a uniform dark brown.

In summer the attractive red squirrel has bright chestnut fur with orange-brown feet and lower legs. Its ears are tufted, but tufts may be smaller or absent in young animals. As summer progresses, the squirrel's bushy tail bleaches to a pale cream. About 8 in. (20 cm) head and body; 7 in. (18 cm) tail.

Red squirrel *Sciurus vulgaris*

Red squirrels are most likely to be seen in heavily forested areas soon after dawn. Mature Scots pine woods are a favourite habitat, but they are also found among other conifers such as larch and spruce. These trees provide a high thoroughfare among the branches and year-round food from cone seeds, buds, shoots and pollen, although the squirrels also like to forage for nuts and acorns among nearby deciduous trees.

The Scots pine was the only large native conifer to survive the last Ice Age, and the red squirrel one of the last mammals to colonise Britain before it was cut off from the rest of Europe some 9,000 years ago. Until the 1940s the animal was fairly widespread. Now it has disappeared from large areas of the country and its place has been taken by the grey squirrel. The reasons for the red squirrel's decline are not clear. One cause may be the extensive loss of suitable woodland, as well as the forestry practice of clear-felling large areas of conifers. It is unlikely that grey squirrels drive away red squirrels, but they may stop them repopulating wooded areas. Red squirrels live for about three years. Few predators can catch them in the trees; on the ground they may be killed by foxes, birds of prey or cars.

Notes and Sketches

A loud churring noise in the tree-tops often reveals the presence of grey squirrels as they aggressively scold or chase off an intruder.

White squirrels are fairly common, in the south-east especially. They have pink eyes and are true albinos.

Silky black squirrels are sometimes seen, although rare. They are found mainly in and around Bedfordshire, where black varieties from North America were released early this century.

Agile grey squirrels can run along slender twigs and leap from tree to tree. Young ones soon learn to do so. If they fall they can land safely from heights of about 30 ft (9 m).

Squirrels are active by day. They like to sit upright on vantage points to survey their surroundings, relying as much on eyesight as smell for information.

Winter fur is dense and a bright, silvery grey with a brown tinge along the middle of the back. It is replaced by brownish summer fur during April and May.

Notes and Sketches

Bushy, grizzled tail

No ear tufts

SITES GUIDE

Squirrels are among the few animals which are active during the day. In picnic areas they quickly become tame. You may see their dreys in trees – these resemble twiggy birds' nests, but the squirrel uses sticks with leaves still attached. You should see grey squirrels at 3–5, 8, 9, 11, 13, 14, 16, 19–22, 24–27, 29, 31–38, 58, 65.

Yellowish-brown fur

In summer the grey squirrel's fur is often yellowish-brown, on the flanks and feet especially. It has a bushy, grizzled tail that stays the same colour all year, white underparts, and ears without tufts. About 10 in. (25 cm) head and body, 8 in. (20 cm) tail.

Common in forests, gardens, hedgerows: scarce on high ground. Range expanding.

Silvery winter fur begins to grow in autumn, starting on the rump. The complete moult takes up to six weeks.

Grey squirrel *Sciurus carolinensis*

One of Britain's most familiar and frequently seen mammals, the grey squirrel is a native of the hardwood forests of the eastern United States. It was introduced to this country in the mid-19th century, but did not become established in the wild until about the turn of the century, after many releases.

Unlike native red squirrels, grey squirrels can live happily in hedgerow trees, parkland, gardens and other places without large areas of trees. Britain's patchwork countryside with dotted trees and isolated copses suited them well and they became abundant. Where grey squirrels spread to live alongside red squirrels, the greys usually became more numerous after a while and displaced their smaller cousins, generally without obvious signs of conflict.

As well as nuts, acorns, beech-mast and fungi, grey squirrels eat tree bark, leaves, shoots, buds and flowers. In commercial woodlands they damage valuable trees and are a serious pest. Elsewhere most people find their behaviour attractive and endearing. Because the squirrels have few predators, some live for up to 10 years. But most die much younger, from starvation, accidents such as forest fires or as a result of pest control.

Notes and Sketches

55

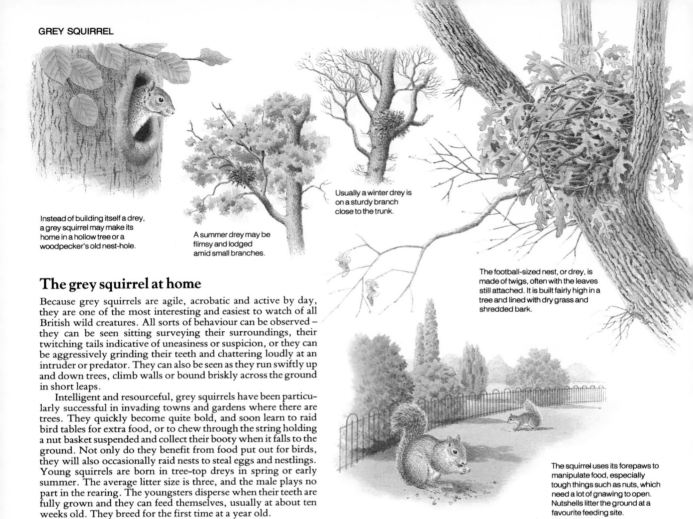

Instead of building itself a drey, a grey squirrel may make its home in a hollow tree or a woodpecker's old nest-hole.

A summer drey may be flimsy and lodged amid small branches.

Usually a winter drey is on a sturdy branch close to the trunk.

The football-sized nest, or drey, is made of twigs, often with the leaves still attached. It is built fairly high in a tree and lined with dry grass and shredded bark.

The squirrel uses its forepaws to manipulate food, especially tough things such as nuts, which need a lot of gnawing to open. Nutshells litter the ground at a favourite feeding site.

The grey squirrel at home

Because grey squirrels are agile, acrobatic and active by day, they are one of the most interesting and easiest to watch of all British wild creatures. All sorts of behaviour can be observed – they can be seen sitting surveying their surroundings, their twitching tails indicative of uneasiness or suspicion, or they can be aggressively grinding their teeth and chattering loudly at an intruder or predator. They can also be seen as they run swiftly up and down trees, climb walls or bound briskly across the ground in short leaps.

Intelligent and resourceful, grey squirrels have been particularly successful in invading towns and gardens where there are trees. They quickly become quite bold, and soon learn to raid bird tables for extra food, or to chew through the string holding a nut basket suspended and collect their booty when it falls to the ground. Not only do they benefit from food put out for birds, they will also occasionally raid nests to steal eggs and nestlings. Young squirrels are born in tree-top dreys in spring or early summer. The average litter size is three, and the male plays no part in the rearing. The youngsters disperse when their teeth are fully grown and they can feed themselves, usually at about ten weeks old. They breed for the first time at a year old.

Notes and Sketches

Strong feet and sharp claws enable grey squirrels to climb brick walls to reach bird food left on upstairs window sills. They will also climb to attics or the roofs of outbuildings to nest.

Squirrels soon master the art of reaching a basket of nuts put out for birds, even if it is suspended by wire from a clothes line.

Tree bark is gnawed to get at the nutritious sapwood below. The raw scar left on the tree may lead to distorted growth and encourage fungal attack.

In late winter, courting squirrels often frisk and chase across lawns or along branches and logs. They run fast, with their tails flicking and their legs outstretched.

Surplus food is stored for winter by burying. Often the cached food is not recovered, and acorns and other seeds sprout the following year, so aiding tree dispersal.

Notes and Sketches

Dark eye rings

Grey body fur

Bushy
grey-brown
tail

The bushy-tailed fat dormouse looks like a small grey squirrel. Its belly is white, and its fine grey body fur often has darker, brownish tinges on the tail, the outside of the legs and in a ring round each eye. About 6 in. (15 cm) head and body, 5 in. (12·5 cm) tail.

Grey
squirrel

Fat
dormouse

Mainly confined to woodland in the Chilterns. It often winters in houses and sheds.

Although the fat dormouse may sit up like a squirrel, it keeps its tail laid flat. Fat dormice come out only at night, and grey squirrels are active only during the day.

Sites Guide

Unless it is introduced to another area of the British Isles, the fat dormouse is unlikely to spread from its present range. Not only is the animal fairly indolent, rarely straying far from its nest, but its present location is bounded by rivers and roads which prevent further colonisation. Fat dormice have not been recorded at any of the sites in this book.

Fat dormouse *Glis glis*

The Romans used to keep fat dormice in captivity and deliberately overfeed them to make a succulent and unusual meal, so they are also known as edible dormice. In the wild these squirrel–like dormice eat extra food in late summer to fatten themselves and build up reserves for the winter.

The fat dormouse was not introduced to Britain until recent times. A few were brought from the Continent, where they are common, and released at Tring in Hertfordshire in 1902. Now they are found in many woodland and suburban areas of the Chilterns, and although in some places they are numerous enough to be regarded as pests, they have not spread very much. The fat dormouse is not a great wanderer and rarely seems to travel more than a few hundred yards from its nest. It spends most of its time high in tree branches, foraging only at night, so is not often seen. But signs of its activity are more evident; it damages trees by chewing bark, buds and growing shoots, and in autumn may enter a house or shed and gnaw woodwork or stored food. It also comes indoors to a dry place to hibernate, and may keep people awake by scuttling about in the loft. It makes little other noise except some squeaks and growls.

Notes and Sketches

Orange-yellow fur

Secretive, nocturnal and rarely seen, the common dormouse is distinguished from all other mice by its fluffy tail, orange-yellow fur and chubby build. It also has smaller ears than other mice, but much bigger eyes than voles. Its belly fur is creamy-white. About 3 in. (75 mm) head and body, 2½ in. (64 mm) tail.

Fluffy tail

Sites Guide

The presence of dormice is difficult to detect because they are both secretive and strictly nocturnal. At night they often spend many hours feeding in the tops of trees. They will eat oak flowers in the spring and ash keys in the autumn, moving about high in the canopy to obtain their food. Dormice have been recorded at 3, 8, 11, 17, 19, 21, 23, 24.

Common dormouse *Muscardinus avellanarius*

In times gone by, the common dormouse was a familiar animal to country folk, and frequently kept as a pet. It was also called the hazel dormouse because it was often found in hazel coppices. Yet today common dormice are rarely encountered, and no one is sure whether this is because they have become rare and threatened, or are merely overlooked. In the days when men spent many hours hedging and ditching – trimming hedges and cleaning out ditches – many a drowsy, hibernating dormouse was exposed, for these tasks were carried out mainly in winter. Many dormouse nests were also discovered when the poles were harvested from coppiced trees. Today these tasks, if done at all, are usually performed by machines, so the presence of dormice is much less likely to be noticed.

In summer dormice live in woodland shrubs and bushes or among tall hedges or dense scrub. They come out only at night to feed on insects, nuts and flowers, so are rarely seen. As they stay hidden among the branches they are not often caught by cats, nor do they normally venture into traps. Dormice may be taken by crows, magpies, owls and foxes, but can live to be about four years old in the wild. Some pets have lived to be six.

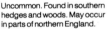

Uncommon. Found in southern hedges and woods. May occur in parts of northern England.

An agile climber, the dormouse will live in a bird's nest-box, even one fixed 12 ft (3-6 m) above the ground.

Notes and Sketches

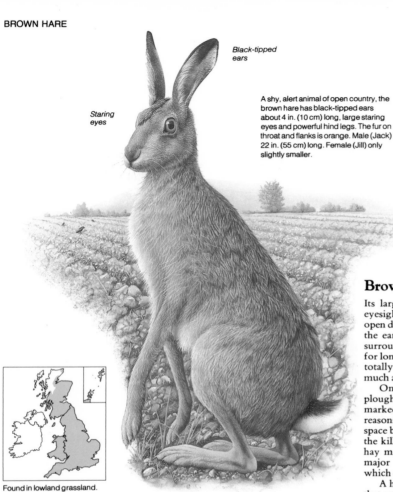

Black-tipped ears

Staring eyes

A shy, alert animal of open country, the brown hare has black-tipped ears about 4 in. (10 cm) long, large staring eyes and powerful hind legs. The fur on throat and flanks is orange. Male (Jack) 22 in. (55 cm) long. Female (Jill) only slightly smaller.

Found in lowland grassland. Widespread but declining. Introduced into Ireland.

SITES GUIDE

A disturbed hare can run as fast as 35 miles an hour to escape from predators. It spends its day lying in grass or in a ploughed field where it appears no more than another clod of earth. Its young are born fully furred and with their eyes open – ready to run. You may see hares at 8, 11, 12, 14, 16, 25, 26, 33 – 35, 37, 38, 43, 47 – 49, 69.

Brown hare *Lepus capensis*

Its large eyes and long ears provide the hare with excellent eyesight and hearing to give it plenty of warning of danger in the open downs or farmland it inhabits. The best time to see one is in the early morning or late evening as it sits up to survey its surroundings. Even when feeding it rarely keeps its head down for long. No other British mammal is better able to survive in a totally open habitat, where cold, windy or rainy weather is as much a challenge to survival as eluding predators.

Once brown hares were a common sight in pastures and ploughed fields, but in recent years numbers have declined markedly although they are still common in Scotland. The reasons for the decline probably include a decrease in living space because of housing developments and new roads, and also the killing of young hares (leverets) by farm machines such as hay mowers and perhaps by insecticides sprayed on crops. A major threat is the use of weedkillers in hay and cornfields, which deprive hares of many plants needed for a nutritious diet.

A hare may live for three or four years – some may be twice that age. Predators such as foxes, owls and buzzards take a few leverets, but adults are fast enough to elude most enemies.

Notes and Sketches

The mountain hare turns wholly or partially white in winter. It is smaller than the brown hare, with a greyer coat, and its ears are also shorter – about 3 in. (75 mm) long. The tail is all white. Usually hares are seen alone or in pairs. About 20 in. (50 cm) long.

Patchy winter coat

Common on upland heather moors, but found at all altitudes in Ireland.

SITES GUIDE

A major fascination about the mountain hare is its ability to change the colour of its coat for the winter. The moult usually takes place in October and the hare will stay white until the spring when it turns brown again. A third moult takes place in the early summer when its coat becomes blue-grey. Look for mountain hares at 38, 50, 53–58, 60, 63, 64.

Mountain hare *Lepus timidus*

High heather moors are the chief home of the mountain hare, and heather is its main food. Because of the blue-grey tinge to its summer coat, it is also known as the blue hare. In summer its all-white tail helps to distinguish it from the rabbit and the brown hare, both of which have dark tops to their tails. The mountain hare's dense white winter coat is more likely to turn wholly white in colder temperatures or at higher altitudes.

The hares feed mostly at night, resting during the day in a scraped hollow or a form nibbled out among the heather. On mountain-sides they tend to move downhill to feed, returning to high ground to rest. In winter they move down from the highest areas to shelter in hollows or hide among boulders, and some 20 or more animals may gather in the same area. Mountain hares breed between February and August and may have three litters a year, each usually with one or two leverets. In some years more than three-quarters of the population dies before the next breeding season. Some may live to be ten years old.

In Ireland, mountain hares replace brown hares, living in all sorts of country including lowland pastures, and are often known as Irish hares. They used to be depicted on Irish coins.

Notes and Sketches

Orange nape

Grey-brown fur

Short tail

Common. Increasing in many areas. Found mainly in farmland, lowland forests.

Rabbits generally have greyish-brown fur with orange at the nape, and a short tail that is black on top and white underneath. They are smaller than hares and have shorter ears without big black tips. Male (buck) 19 in. (48 cm) long. Female (doe) smaller with a narrower head.

SITES GUIDE

Subordinate female rabbits give birth to their young away from the main warren in a short dead-end burrow called a 'stop'. The doe excavates this and lines it with grasses and fur from her own coat to give her babies a comfortable bed. Look for rabbits at most of the sites in this book.

Rabbit *Oryctolagus cuniculus*

It was not until the 12th century that there were rabbits in Britain. They were introduced from the Continent as a valuable source of meat and skins. For long they remained a profitable part of the rural economy, but in the last 200 years have become major agricultural pests.

Rabbits are sociable creatures and live in colonies in burrow systems known as warrens, where a status system rules. Dominant rabbits, either male or female, claim and mark a territory in the best part of the warren and are more successful at breeding than subordinate rabbits. A subordinate does not establish a territory, and mixes amicably with other subordinates. But if it enters the territory of a dominant individual, it is driven off.

Most rabbit activity takes place at night and close to the warren. The animals rarely move more than 150 yds (about 140 metres) away from home, so the vegetation near the warren is kept short by frequent grazing. This leaves a wide, open area for revealing the approach of predators – rabbits have a good sense of smell and hearing and their prominent eyes are set so that they can see all ways at once. Short vegetation also helps the rabbits to keep their fur dry.

Notes and Sketches

Broad wings

Its large size and broad, rounded wings distinguish the greater horseshoe bat. It gets its name from the horseshoe-shaped skin (nose-leaf) – used for echo-location – round its nostrils. Female 2½ in. (64 mm) head and body, 13½ in. (34 cm) wingspan. Male smaller.

Declining. Found only where suitable hibernation places and conditions still exist.

Greater horseshoe bat *Rhinolophus ferrumequinum*

Once common in southern Britain, greater horseshoe bats are now scarce and in danger of extinction. Like other bats, they have suffered considerably from the decline in the number of places where insects abound – such as hedges, ponds and old grassland – as well as from eating insects contaminated with pesticides. Another handicap is that southern Britain is the extreme northern limit of the greater horseshoe bats' range. They really prefer a warmer climate. If there are several cold or wet summers in succession, the bats do not breed very successfully and the young have difficulty in surviving their first year.

Greater horseshoe bats also need to find somewhere for winter hibernation – large, spacious, humid places such as old mines, caves or damp tunnels – and their numbers and distribution are limited by the availability of such places. Even where suitable places exist they may be frequently disturbed or be blocked up for safety. Efforts have been made to protect the bats' favourite breeding and hibernation sites and, like other British bats, they are protected by law. But these measures may not be enough to save a species whose numbers have shrunk to probably less than a quarter of what they were 20 years ago.

Notes and Sketches

Broad
wings

SITES GUIDE

Horseshoe bats do not creep
into crevices to roost or
hibernate but hang from any
suitable protrusion. This may
be a nail or the edge of
roofing felt in a roof used as
a summer roost, or it can be
any kind of irregularity in a
cellar or cave onto which
their feet can grip. Like all
bats, lesser horseshoes are
protected and may not be
disturbed.

Found where there are caves
or mines for hibernation. A few
recorded from east England.

The lesser horseshoe bat has a body
smaller than a man's thumb, and is one
of Britain's tiniest mammals. Like the
greater horseshoe bat, it has a nose-leaf
(horseshoe-shaped skin round the
nostrils), a rounded body and broad wings.
Female 1½ in. (40 mm) head and body,
10 in. (25 cm) wingspan. Male smaller.

Lesser horseshoe bat *Rhinolophus hipposideros*

The lesser horseshoe bat is a delicate, very much smaller edition
of the greater horseshoe bat, and more often solitary. Like its
large, robust cousin, the bat likes to hibernate in damp cellars,
mines or tunnels in winter, so lives only where such places are
available. Because of its smaller size, however, its choice is less
restricted, for it can fly in a tunnel only 6 in. (15 cm) high, or up
a shaft only 20 in. (50 cm) wide. In Britain lesser horseshoe bats
do not seem to travel very far from their regular haunts, but
on the Continent journeys of up to 95 miles (150 km) have
been recorded.

The bats mate in autumn and winter, but the embryo does
not begin to develop until April. A female produces only one
baby a year, born usually in July or August in an attic, a hollow
tree or an old building. Youngsters can fly around the roost
when three weeks old, and all can look after themselves by late
August. Young bats do not normally breed until their second
year. Although a lesser horseshoe bat is similar in size to a
common shrew, its life-span is probably four or five times
longer. Winter hibernation may save the bat from some of the
wear and tear experienced by the ever-active shrew.

Notes and Sketches

Short,
broad ears

Pipistrelle bat *Pipistrellus pipistrellus*

The tiny pipistrelle is Britain's smallest bat and also the most abundant and widespread. Pipistrelles congregate in large colonies, often in buildings such as churches, and can be heard squeaking before they stream out 15–30 minutes before sunset to forage for insects. Colonies may be very large, numbering 1,000 or more bats. Favourite summer roosting places are small, warm spaces behind tiles on a south-facing tile-hung wall, or behind weather-boarding or wooden shingles. Such features are found on many fairly modern houses and bungalows, so pipistrelles may be common in areas with new housing.

Warmth is essential for the tiny young, born mostly in June. They are hairless for a week after birth and liable to become chilled. The warmer they are, the faster they can grow. In summer, mothers and young live in separate colonies from males. Winter colonies contain both sexes, and it is during winter that mating occurs, although fertilisation is delayed until about April. Pipistrelles hibernate from about late November until late March, preferring cool, dry places such as churches, house roofs or old trees. They fly out sometimes during hibernation, occasionally by day.

Common. Widespread in all habitats, cities included. May be rare on high ground.

Pipistrelle bats are very tiny, with short, broad ears and fairly narrow wings. Adults vary in colour from place to place; in some colonies they are mainly orange-brown, in others pale grey-brown. The bats are common in buildings. About 1⅜ in. (35 mm) head and body, 8½ in. (22 cm) wingspan.

Notes and Sketches

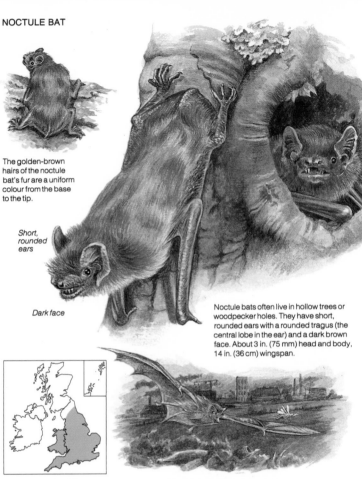

The golden-brown hairs of the noctule bat's fur are a uniform colour from the base to the tip.

Short, rounded ears

Dark face

Noctule bats often live in hollow trees or woodpecker holes. They have short, rounded ears with a rounded tragus (the central lobe in the ear) and a dark brown face. About 3 in. (75 mm) head and body, 14 in. (36 cm) wingspan.

Common in southern Britain, especially in the Midlands and south-eastern counties.

Prey is mostly larger insects caught on the wing. The bat will swoop low to catch an insect such as a cricket.

Young are born in June or July. Usually there is only one baby, but females may sometimes have twins.

SITES GUIDE

It is easy to identify a tree hole used as a roost by noctules because there will be a dark streak of urine, faeces and tree sap below the entrance. A pair of binoculars is useful when searching for such bat roosts – especially if the entrance is high. Noctules have been recorded at 17, 18, 25 and 37 but it is illegal to disturb them in any way.

Noctule bat *Nyctalus noctula*

The noctule bat is a powerful and expert flyer, so it is strange that, although common in much of England and Wales, it is not found in Ireland or most of Scotland. It is one of the largest British bats and could easily fly across the Irish Sea. On the Continent, noctule bats regularly migrate hundreds of miles.

High-flying noctule bats are often on the wing before dark in summer, swooping after insects among swifts and martins. They are mostly tree dwellers, roosting in colonies in tree-holes in parks and woods, although they will sometimes use a house roof. If a roost becomes too hot or too crowded, they move to another. Noctules may have difficulty in finding roosts, because nesting starlings take over many suitable tree-holes.

Like most bats, noctules form nursery roosts of females and young in summer. The young are born in June or July and weaned at about a month old. In winter, from about October until the end of March, the bats hibernate in trees and buildings. They do not use caves, where temperatures are more stable, which suggests that they can stand low temperatures better than most other bats. Noctules probably live for ten years or more, and have few predators.

Notes and Sketches

SITES GUIDE

Although this bat has been recorded as a tree dweller, it has been observed roosting in buildings in recent years. Leisler's bat seems to have two periods of hunting activity, one shortly after sunset and the other which ends about half an hour before sunrise. Leisler's bat is protected and may not be disturbed, but one has been recorded at 45.

Short, rounded ears

Broad muzzle

In summer adult males gather in small groups and live apart from the females and young.

Patchily distributed. May be uncommon. In Ireland it replaces the noctule bat.

Leisler's bat is very similar to the noctule bat, with short, rounded ears and a broad muzzle. Although it is smaller than the noctule and has slightly darker fur with paler tips, it is hard to tell the two bats apart. About 2½ in. (64 mm) head and body, 12 in. (30 cm) wingspan.

Leisler's bat *Nyctalus leisleri*

Leisler's bat is also known as the lesser noctule bat, and is very similar to the noctule. It differs only in its smaller size and the fact that its glossy bronze fur is paler at the tip rather than a uniform colour throughout. Both species are high flyers, often about before sunset, but have a curiously different distribution. Leisler's bat is present in Ireland, where there are apparently no noctules. But in Great Britain it has been recorded only rarely, and then in widely separated localities.

Like the noctule, Leisler's bat has a short, very broad muzzle and a semi–circular tragus (central ear lobe) – features not found in other species of British bats. It is a tree dweller, roosting in tree–holes in summer and hibernating in them in winter – from about October until the end of March. Nesting starlings probably deprive Leisler's bats of many suitable roosting holes, added to which they also have to compete for them with the larger noctules. Little is known about the Leisler's breeding habits but, like noctules, the females probably each produce one baby a year in June or July, rearing them in nursery roosts. Leisler's bats have few creatures preying on them and their normal life–span is probably ten years or more.

Notes and Sketches

Grizzled fur

Dark face and ears

Common in parts of southern and eastern England. A few isolated sightings in north.

The serotine is a large bat with powerful jaws, a dark face and ears and a pointed tragus (the central lobe in the ear). Its brown fur is paler at the tips, making it look grizzled. About 2½ in. (64 mm) head and body, 14 in. (36 cm) wingspan.

SITES GUIDE

Serotines often live in old brick houses, gaining access to the roof space at the gable end. These bats can catch and eat large moths or beetles in flight. A serotine has been timed eating a cockchafer beetle in a little over a minute and a half, discarding only the hard wing cases and legs. This species is protected and may be seen at 17.

Serotine bat *Eptesicus serotinus*

Although it is a large bat and a strong flyer, the serotine has a surprisingly localised distribution. It is common only in certain areas of southern and eastern England, especially in the south-east, and where it occurs, it is the large bat most often seen. There are hardly any records of serotine bats being seen to the north or west of the Midlands.

Serotines particularly like to raise their young in the attics of old houses, often hanging up along the roof ridge. Unlike the tiny pipistrelle bat, they are too large to squeeze behind slates and tiles. Colonies may return to the same place year after year, causing an accumulation of small, very black droppings in the roof space. These differ from rat or mouse droppings in containing shiny pieces of chewed insects, and although they can be smelly they are not a health hazard. Nursing colonies can be quite noisy and may be unpopular with householders, but it is illegal to disturb them. In any case, once the young are able to look after themselves – usually about August – the colony departs. They spend the winter elsewhere, hibernating in another roof or a hollow tree. Serotines probably live for about five years. Some may survive to be 15 or more.

Notes and Sketches

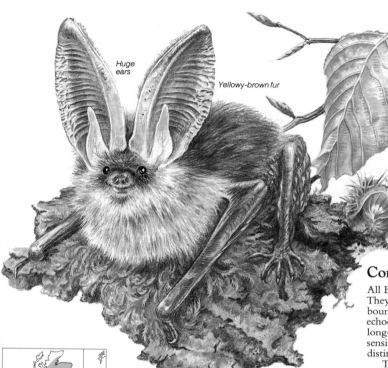

Huge
ears

Yellowy-brown fur

SITES GUIDE

Otherwise known as the
brown long-eared bat, this
mammal folds its ears back
when at rest, so that they
look like a pair of ram's
horns. In hibernation, to
reduce moisture loss, the
ears are folded down
alongside the body and
tucked under the wings. You
may see these bats at 3, 17,
33, 45, 47–49, 57, 67.

Found in woods, house roofs.
Widespread, but not in open,
exposed places or far north.

Huge oval ears meeting at the base
distinguish the long-eared bat. The ears
are about 1⅛ in. (28 mm) long, nearly
three-quarters of the length of the head
and body. The bat has broad wings and
yellowy or light brown fur, paler below.
About 1¾ in. (45 mm) head and body,
10 in. (25 cm) wingspan.

Common long-eared bat *Plecotus auritus*

All British bats use their hearing to navigate and to locate food.
They emit sound – too high-pitched for human ears – that
bounces back from obstacles, including tiny insects. From these
echoes a bat learns the distance and direction of an object. The
long-eared bat's huge ears are part of a system of echo-location
sensitive enough not only to detect flying insects, but also to
distinguish between an insect or larva and the leaf it is on.

The long-eared bat can also fly with fine control in small
spaces. This, together with its refined echo-location, enables it
to thread its way through tree branches and foliage and even
hover above a leaf to pick off an insect. It is principally a
woodland bat that roosts in trees, although it often breeds in
attics. Long-eared bats hibernate, usually alone, from about
November to March. Sometimes they hibernate in the summer
roost, which is unusual among bats, but commonly seek out a
different place to spend the winter, such as a cave or mine. Some
live for 12 years or more. The common long-eared bat differs
from the rare grey long-eared bat in colour. It has yellowish-
tipped pale brown fur, whereas the grey has darker fur with
hairs dark grey at the base.

Notes and Sketches

Although a barbastelle usually alights head up, it may twist round before attaching itself to hang head down from a wall or tree-trunk.

Frosted coat

Short, broad ears

Pug-like face

The distinctive barbastelle bat has a pug-like face with a bare, dark brown snout and short, broad ears that meet between the eyes. The glossy fur is almost black, and on older bats is cream tipped, giving them a frosted look. About 1¾ in. (45 mm) head and body. 10½ in. (27 cm) wingspan.

Found only in the southern half of Great Britain, but elusive and rarely seen.

The ears are almost as broad as they are long, and have a stiffening fold at the front. There is a long, pointed tragus (central ear lobe).

SITES GUIDE

Like the Leisler's bat, the barbastelle generally has two periods of activity at night. It flies reasonably fast, sometimes with slow wingbeats. The barbastelle tends to be an individualist and is rarely found in groups. These bats are protected and have not been recorded at any of the sites in this book.

Barbastelle bat *Barbastella barbastellus*

No other British bat bears any resemblance to the strange-looking barbastelle, with its squashed face, thick black ears that meet between the eyes and long, frosted-looking, blackish fur. It is so peculiar that there is only one other species like it in the world, another barbastelle found in the Middle East and Asia.

Barbastelles seem to be uncommon, because despite their distinctive looks, sightings are rarely reported. They are found in open woodland, especially in river valleys, where they fly low over the water and are active intermittently through the night. As with all bats, the males are smaller than the females and tend to be solitary, leaving the females to form nursery colonies in summer to raise their young. In winter, barbastelles have been found hibernating in caves and ornamental grottoes with other bats, but only in the coldest weather. They tend to choose the coolest places to hibernate, which suggests that they are hardy and able to tolerate low temperatures so can normally spend the winter in relatively unsheltered sites. Although in Britain the barbastelle has been recorded mainly in the south, on the Continent it is found as far north as latitude 60° and eastwards into Russia. It can live for at least 18 years.

Notes and Sketches

White underside

Natterer's bat has a distinctive pure white underside, and its tail membranes are baggy with outward-curving edges. Its ears are drooping and rather long, and its face long and reddish with a bare, narrow muzzle. About 1¾ in. (45 mm) head and body, 11 in. (28 cm) wingspan.

Common. Widespread in woods, farmland and parkland. Not found in northern Scotland.

When the bat crawls, the distinct dividing line between its light brown upper parts and white underside shows clearly.

The ears droop sideways and have distinctive upturned tips, which are darker than the pinkish bases. If laid forwards they extend well beyond the bat's nostrils.

Natterer's bat *Myotis nattereri*

Natterer's bat is named after its discoverer, an early 19th-century Austrian naturalist. It is most easily recognised by its pure white underside as it flies slowly and often at rooftop height soon after sunset, searching for small flying insects such as moths. It will sometimes pick insects off foliage. In flight the bat often holds its tail pointing downwards instead of trailing to the rear, as is usual in other bats. Along the edge of each tail membrane there are about ten tiny, bead-like swellings, each sprouting a short, very fine hair that is scarcely visible. The function of this fringe is unknown; Natterer's is the only bat species with such a feature.

In summer, breeding colonies of females and young gather in hollow trees or house roofs. As with many other bats, the females bear only one baby in June or early July. It can fly by about August. During their first year, young Natterer's bats can be distinguished from adults by their colouring, being greyish-brown, including their underparts. The bats do not generally hibernate until December, emerging in early March. They hibernate in caves if these are available, but seem content to use hollow trees or other sites. They can live for 25 years.

Notes and Sketches

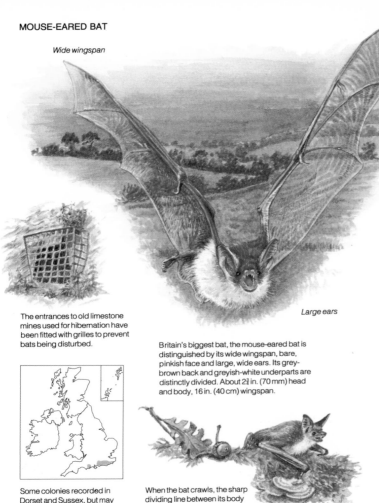

Wide wingspan

Large ears

The entrances to old limestone mines used for hibernation have been fitted with grilles to prevent bats being disturbed.

Britain's biggest bat, the mouse-eared bat is distinguished by its wide wingspan, bare, pinkish face and large, wide ears. Its grey-brown back and greyish-white underparts are distinctly divided. About 2¾ in. (70 mm) head and body, 16 in. (40 cm) wingspan.

A nursery roost may be in a warm dry attic or an old railway tunnel.

Some colonies recorded in Dorset and Sussex, but may now be extinct in Britain.

When the bat crawls, the sharp dividing line between its body colours shows clearly.

SITES GUIDE

Sadly for the mouse-eared bat, the legislation protecting it from disturbance appears to have been enacted too late. Recent records have indicated only two mouse-eared bats existing in Britain – both males. Mouse-eared bats do not occur at any of the properties in this book.

Mouse-eared bat *Myotis myotis*

Its slow, heavy flight and large wingspan – almost one–third larger than that of any other British species – easily distinguishes the mouse-eared bat. It is the biggest bat known in this country, but may now be extinct in Britain. Because of its scarcity it has had legal protection since 1975.

On the Continent mouse-eared bats are fairly common in places, and sometimes form large colonies. In Britain the only known regular haunts have been in Sussex and Dorset, and it is possible that these bats had in fact flown across the Channel from France, although no one has yet proved that such flights take place. For a mouse-eared bat seeking a suitable place to spend the winter, the short flight from France to England might be well worth the effort. In eastern Europe mouse-eared bats are known to travel 125 miles (200 km) or more between their summer and winter quarters. Mouse-eared bats seem to prefer open woodland or farming country. In summer the females give birth to their single young in a warm dry place such as an attic, and the males live alone elsewhere. The winter is often spent in the cool, sheltered conditions of a cave or an old mine tunnel. The bats can live for 15 years or more.

Notes and Sketches

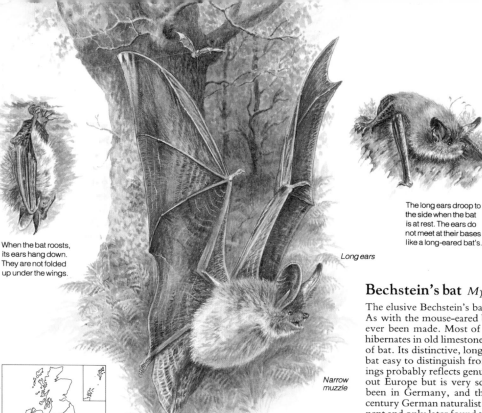

When the bat roosts, its ears hang down. They are not folded up under the wings.

The long ears droop to the side when the bat is at rest. The ears do not meet at their bases like a long-eared bat's.

Long ears

Narrow muzzle

Found only in the extreme south of England, but even there very rarely seen.

Next to the long-eared bat, the rare Bechstein's bat has the longest ears of any bat in Europe – they measure about 1 in. (25 mm). Its muzzle is pinkish-brown and fairly long and narrow. About 1¾ in. (45 mm) head and body, 11 in. (28 cm) wingspan.

Bechstein's bat *Myotis bechsteini*

The elusive Bechstein's bat is one of Britain's rarest mammals. As with the mouse-eared bat, only a few dozen sightings have ever been made. Most of these have been in Dorset, where it hibernates in old limestone mines along with several other kinds of bat. Its distinctive, long-eared appearance makes Bechstein's bat easy to distinguish from other species, so the lack of sightings probably reflects genuine scarcity. The bat ranges throughout Europe but is very scarce there too. Most sightings have been in Germany, and the bat is named after an early 19th-century German naturalist. It was first discovered on the Continent and only later found to occur in Britain.

Bechstein's bat seems to be a woodland species that frequents parkland, often flying about 10 ft (3 m) above the ground, and roosts in hollow trees. Its bones have been found in old flint mines that date back to the Stone Age, when most of southern Britain was covered by extensive forests. Like other bats, female Bechstein's give birth to one baby a year. The nursery roost is often in an attic or tree-hole. The bat probably feeds mostly on moths, sometimes other insects, taking them mainly in flight but occasionally off a leaf surface.

Notes and Sketches

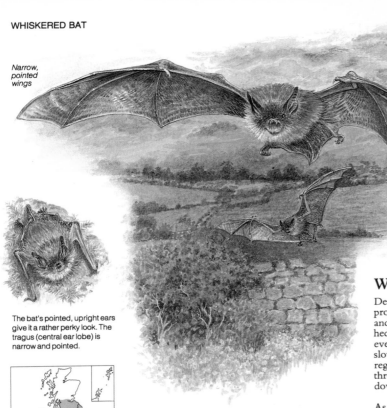

Narrow, pointed wings

Tiny feet

The bat's pointed, upright ears give it a rather perky look. The tragus (central ear lobe) is narrow and pointed.

Widespread except in far north. Probably found in Ireland, but not recorded.

Whiskered bats are small and delicate, with narrow, pointed wings and tiny feet. The muzzle is narrow and the face and ears very dark, especially in young animals in their first year which also have darker underparts than adults. About 1½ in. (40 mm) head and body, 9½ in. (24 cm) wingspan.

SITES GUIDE

Whiskered bats have been seen flying during the day in late winter and spring. Birds of prey occasionally capture bats who do this, although it is an unusual occurrence and the major threats to bats as a whole come from man. Whiskered bats have been recorded at 17, 35, 37.

Whiskered bat *Myotis mystacinus*

Despite its name, the whiskered bat does not have particularly prominent whiskers, but it does have more fur round the eyes and muzzle than most other bats. Common around buildings, hedges or woodland fringes, the bat may be seen from early evening – usually alone but occasionally in groups as it makes slow, fluttering flights in search of insects. Usually it follows a regular track repeatedly before moving elsewhere. It is active through the night but probably rests at times, hanging upside down against tree bark or some other rough surface.

Whiskered bats hibernate in cool places from late autumn. As with most other bats, mating takes place during short periods of wakefulness in winter. The females are therefore pregnant as soon as (or soon after) they come out of hibernation in early spring, allowing the single young to be born as early as possible in summer – usually about June. They then have plenty of time to feed, grow and fatten up before winter, when food supplies become insufficient for normal activity. Tiny whiskered bats can live for about 19 years. Although they do not seem to travel far in Britain, on the Continent marked bats have been known to journey some 1,200 miles (nearly 2,000 kilometres).

Notes and Sketches

SITES GUIDE

Canals seem to be a favourite place of Daubenton's bats. They roost in the tunnels or under bridges and emerge early in the evening to skim up and down over the surface of the water in search of prey. Daubenton's bats have been noted at 3, 25, 37, 45, 62.

Large feet

The bat's short ears are wider than those of the whiskered bat, and paler at the base.

Daubenton's bat is often called the water bat because of its tendency to fly very low over water. It has short ears and a short, broad, pinkish-brown muzzle. The large feet with splayed toes are distinctive. About 1¾ in. (45 mm) head and body, 10 in. (25 cm) wingspan.

Widespread in most parts of Britain except the far north and exposed places.

To hibernate, a bat may crawl backwards into a crevice in a cave, wall, rock-face or hollow tree.

Daubenton's bat *Myotis daubentoni*

When it skims low over a pond or lake at night, Daubenton's bat uses shallow, fluttering wing-beats that enable it to get very close to the surface. In this way it can pick up mayflies as they emerge from the water, and may also manage to catch other aquatic insects, plankton and even small fish occasionally – a food source not exploited by other British bats. Daubenton's bat is widespread and usually found not far from trees or water. It does not always hunt low; it may be seen flying fairly high and it is most likely to be confused with the whiskered bat. At close quarters, however, its large feet distinguish it.

When hunting, a Daubenton's bat often patrols repeatedly up and down a regular beat, then moves to another. These favoured beats may actually be defended from other bats, but little is known of bats' territorial and social behaviour because of the difficulty of studying them in flight and in the dark. Like other bats, Daubenton's females bear one baby a year about June or July. Nursery roosts, with no adult males present, are often in buildings and sometimes contain scores of bats. During the winter, Daubenton's bats tend to be solitary, hibernating alone in caves or trees.

Notes and Sketches

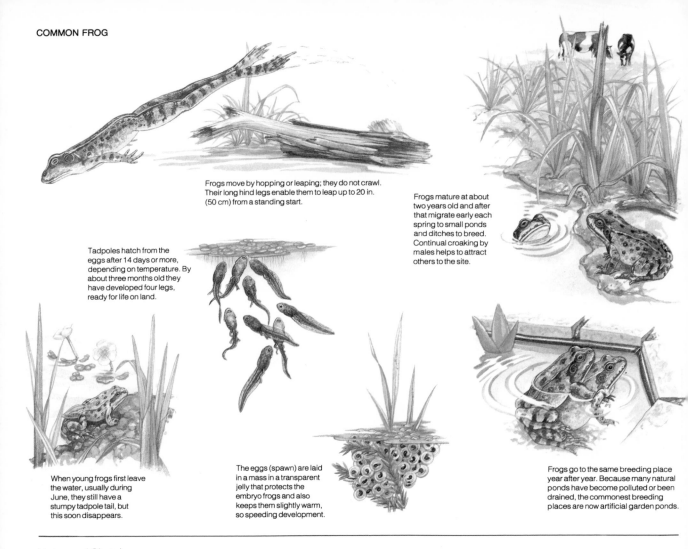

Frogs move by hopping or leaping; they do not crawl. Their long hind legs enable them to leap up to 20 in. (50 cm) from a standing start.

Frogs mature at about two years old and after that migrate early each spring to small ponds and ditches to breed. Continual croaking by males helps to attract others to the site.

Tadpoles hatch from the eggs after 14 days or more, depending on temperature. By about three months old they have developed four legs, ready for life on land.

When young frogs first leave the water, usually during June, they still have a stumpy tadpole tail, but this soon disappears.

The eggs (spawn) are laid in a mass in a transparent jelly that protects the embryo frogs and also keeps them slightly warm, so speeding development.

Frogs go to the same breeding place year after year. Because many natural ponds have become polluted or been drained, the commonest breeding places are now artificial garden ponds.

Notes and Sketches

Dark patch
behind eye

Variable
skin colour

The common frog lives on land in damp places for most of the year, often blending well with its surroundings. The dark patch behind its eye is distinctive, but body colour varies widely from dark greenish-grey to chestnut or yellow, or sometimes albino. Female about 3 in. (75 mm) head and body. Male slightly smaller.

Widespread in wet habitats, but land drainage is making it increasingly scarce.

SITES GUIDE

Once tadpoles have hatched, they take about three months to grow into tiny frogs, emerging from the water still with the remnants of their tadpole tails. It will be two years, though, before they mature and return to the pond of their birth to breed. Frogs are very common and may be seen at 8, 9, 24, 26– 29, 31–35, 37, 38, 41, 42, 45, 48, 50–53, 64, 68.

Common frog *Rana temporaria*

Open woods and lush pastures are typically the home of the common frog, which likes moist places not too far from water. But frogs are becoming increasingly common in gardens with ponds, and it is not unusual to find a hundred or more using a pond for spawning. As frogs eat insects and small animals such as slugs and snails, they are good friends to the gardener. They like to hide in tall vegetation on summer days, and emerge on warm damp nights to hunt.

In winter, from about mid-October, common frogs hibernate in sheltered places on land or in the muddy bottoms of ponds. They emerge to migrate to breeding ponds, often in January in the south-west but usually in February or March in other parts. After spawning frogs usually stay in the water until the weather gets warmer, leaving during April to live on land. When the young frogs emerge in June or July, large numbers are killed by predators such as blackbirds. At any age they may fall prey to a host of animals, including crows, herons, ducks, hedgehogs, rats, foxes, grass snakes and cats. Frogs are now rare in farmland, mainly because of the increase in arable fields treated with pesticides, and the neglect or filling in of ponds.

Notes and Sketches

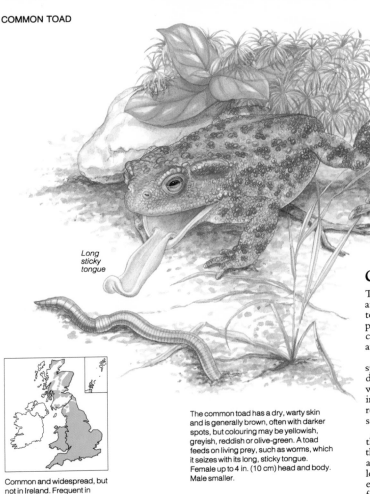

Warty skin

Long sticky tongue

Common toad *Bufo bufo*

Toad migration in March or early April can be a spectacular affair. Within the space of a few days, hundreds of common toads leave their hibernation places and make for their breeding pond, on their way climbing walls and other obstacles and crossing roads in a mass. Many are killed, especially by vehicles, and in some places warning signs are erected on busy roads.

Common toads like to spawn in fairly deep water. Strings of spawn (eggs) are usually about 7–10 ft (2–3 m) long. Eggs develop into tadpoles and then young toads in about 10–16 weeks depending on the weather. Young toads leave the water in June or July, only 1 in 20 surviving to become adult. Males are ready to breed at about three years old and females a year later, so males heavily outnumber females at breeding time.

When spawning is over, adults leave the ponds to live alone through the summer. Most of the day is spent under logs, but the toads emerge in the evening to catch insects and other small animals. They sit and wait for prey to come within range of their long tongue, which is rooted at the front of the mouth and can be extended for nearly 1 in. (25 mm). In captivity toads may live for 20 years, but in the wild not usually more than ten.

The common toad has a dry, warty skin and is generally brown, often with darker spots, but colouring may be yellowish, greyish, reddish or olive-green. A toad feeds on living prey, such as worms, which it seizes with its long, sticky tongue. Female up to 4 in. (10 cm) head and body. Male smaller.

Common and widespread, but not in Ireland. Frequent in gardens, often in dry places.

Notes and Sketches

A yellow line down the middle of its back distinguishes the natterjack toad from the common toad. It is also slightly smaller and has a shinier, smoother skin. Adults vary in colour from yellowish-green to olive-green. Head and body 2½ in. (64 mm).

Yellow stripe

SITES GUIDE

Sand dunes are the habitat of the natterjack toad and the early riser may find their beautiful feathery tracks traced in the dry sand faces after their night's activity. Choose a windless morning and arrive while the sun is still low enough to show the tracks to best advantage. Natterjack toads are a protected species.

Found on sandy heaths and coastal dunes. Common in a few restricted localities.

At breeding time, from March to midsummer, males call loudly to attract females. Each distends its single throat sac to give a penetrating, rattling croak.

Natterjack toad *Bufo calamita*

The name of the natterjack toad is probably derived from the Anglo-Saxon word *naeddre*, which meant a serpent or crawling creature. The addition of 'jack' may refer to the toad's small size, as it does in jack-snipe, for instance. The natterjack is found only in sandy places, mainly in coastal dunes in East Anglia and north-west England, but was once common on southern heathlands. Now its numbers are declining and it is protected by law.

Natterjack toads dig burrows in soft sand, and often shelter there in a group. They generally emerge to forage at night, feeding on insects and other small animals. Winter is spent buried 1–2 ft (30–60 cm) deep in the sand. Spawning begins in April and continues until June or July. During this time the males sit in the water round the edges of the shallow, sandy pools used for breeding and croak loudly. Their night chorus can sometimes be heard more than half a mile (1 km) away. Many tadpoles die because their pond dries up before they become toadlets. Most toadlets leave the water in June or July.

Although natterjack toads have poisonous skins, some predators – seagulls and crows, for example – have learned to eat them leaving the skin untouched. Toads may live 10–12 years.

Notes and Sketches

Newts usually hibernate on land during winter. They often choose a damp cellar or a garden corner, but are never far from water.

Like all newts, common newts are greedy feeders. With their sticky tongues they catch slugs, worms, insects and even other newts. They swallow their prey whole – including snails in their shells.

Great crested newt
Triturus cristatus

The largest British newt, with a slimy, warty skin, blackish above with a black-spotted golden-yellow belly. Males have a high, toothed crest and a silver-streaked tail. The species is declining and is protected by law. About 6¼ in. (16 cm) long including tail.

Palmate newt
Triturus helveticus

The smallest British newt, olive-brown above with a dark streak across the eye. Breeding males have webbed hind feet, a low, smooth crest and a short filament on the tail. About 3 in. (75 mm) long including tail.

The tiny young leave the water at the end of the summer, after they have changed from tadpoles into miniature newts.

At breeding time male common newts have a bright orange underside and spots on the throat as well as the belly. Male palmate newts have a whitish-yellow underside and plain pink throat. The females of the two species are drabber and hard to tell apart.

Notes and Sketches

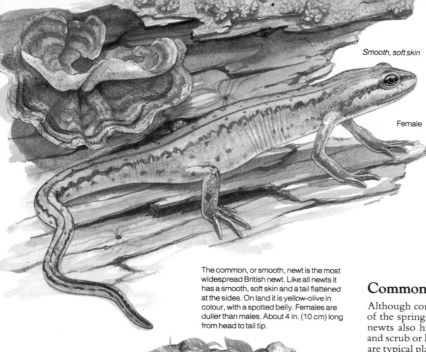

Smooth, soft skin

Female

The common, or smooth, newt is the most widespread British newt. Like all newts it has a smooth, soft skin and a tail flattened at the sides. On land it is yellow-olive in colour, with a spotted belly. Females are duller than males. About 4 in. (10 cm) long from head to tail tip.

Common and widespread, mainly in lowland Britain. The only newt found in Ireland.

A male common newt has a low ridge of skin running along its back in summer, the remains of its spring breeding crest.

Common newt *Triturus vulgaris*

Although common newts live in their breeding pools for most of the spring, they spend summer and autumn on land. Most newts also hibernate on land during winter. Open woodland and scrub or lush pasture, with suitable breeding ponds near by, are typical places to find newts, and they are becoming common in gardens. By day they hide under stones or logs or in thick grass. On damp nights they emerge to hunt for slugs, worms and insects, tracking prey by both sight and scent. Newts look something like lizards but have no scales and move very slowly. They never bask in the sun as lizards do.

Early in spring newts move to the water to breed. The eggs are individually wrapped in water plant leaves. Adults return to land in early summer, leaving the tadpoles to develop into fully formed but tiny newts which emerge to live on land at the end of summer. They stay there until two years old, when they return to the water to breed. Common newts are the most abundant, but palmate newts tend to take over in heathland or uplands. Great crested newts are found in lowland England but are becoming rare. If it escapes predators such as hedgehogs, rats and grass snakes, a newt can live about ten years.

Notes and Sketches

ADDER

Females are usually duller and browner than males, with less contrast between markings and background colouring. They are also fatter, and may be up to 30 in. (76 cm) long.

V marking

Zigzag line

Widespread, but distribution patchy. Found in hedgerows, farmland, open moors, woods.

In spring male adders may be seen 'dancing' (wrestling to win a female). They rear, sway, writhe and race over vegetation as each tries to force the other to the ground. Adders vary in colour and markings, but a dark zigzag line along the back and a V mark on the back of the head are characteristic. Male about 24 in. (60 cm) long. Female often longer.

SITES GUIDE

Adders slide up behind their prey, bite it to inject their venom and retire until the small mammal succumbs. Then they return to swallow their meal whole. Adders are fairly common and you should look for them at 8, 9, 11, 14, 17, 19, 20, 22, 27–29, 31, 33, 37, 45, 49, 52, 53.

Adder *Vipera berus*

According to an old legend, a female adder swallows her young when danger threatens. What actually happens is that the young snakes hide under their mother's belly. The adder, or viper, is Britain's commonest snake and the only one that is poisonous. But it is very timid and normally flees from humans before anyone gets close enough to provoke it into biting. The bite is rarely fatal but needs hospital treatment as soon as possible.

Adders like open places such as heaths, moors and scrub-covered hillsides, and are sometimes found among sand-dunes. They shed their skins from time to time, and cast skins may be a sign of their presence. On farmland they are the farmer's friend, eating small mammals such as mice and voles. They also eat lizards, frogs and toads if nothing else is available, but do not eat every day; a large meal may last a week or more. Male adders emerge from hibernation in February or March, females a little later, and courtship reaches its peak in April. Females usually become pregnant only once every two years. The young are born fully formed in August or September and take two or three years to reach maturity. Adders have few enemies apart from man, and may live for nine or ten years.

Notes and Sketches

Dark spots

Eye stripe

Like all snakes, the smooth snake sheds or sloughs its skin from time to time. This worn outer layer first becomes loose at the head and the snake gradually rubs the skin off in one piece by squeezing between twigs and stiff stems. Smooth snakes are rare and are protected by law. No sites are included in this book.

Very rare. Found on some heaths in southern England. Numbers probably declining.

The smooth snake is slimmer than an adder, with smoother scales. It also has a narrower head with a dark side-stripe through each eye. Colouring varies from grey to brown or red-brown, and there are dark spots down the back, sometimes joined as bars. Up to 24 in. (60 cm) long.

Smooth snake *Coronella austriaca*

Lowland heaths of the type found in Surrey, Hampshire and Dorset are the home of the smooth snake, one of Britain's rarest animals. Because it is so rare it is now protected by law, and whether or not it can continue to exist in Britain depends on how much heathland can be preserved. Lowland heaths are under increasing pressure from farmers and foresters, as well as from walkers and picnickers and the ravages of heath fires.

Because the smooth snake is very shy as well as rare, there is still much to be learned about its way of life. It rarely basks in the open, preferring to get the sun's warmth indirectly by lying under a flat stone or similar objects. In spring, when they emerge from winter hibernation, smooth snakes are sometimes seen basking intertwined among heather. Like many other reptiles, individuals have a particular home range and stay in the same area for a long time. Much of their time is spent burrowing underground, and they mostly eat other reptiles such as lizards. They are also cannibals, at least in captivity.

Mating takes place in May. The young are born in August or September and are self-sufficient from birth. Smooth snakes may survive in the wild for 15–20 years or more.

Notes and Sketches

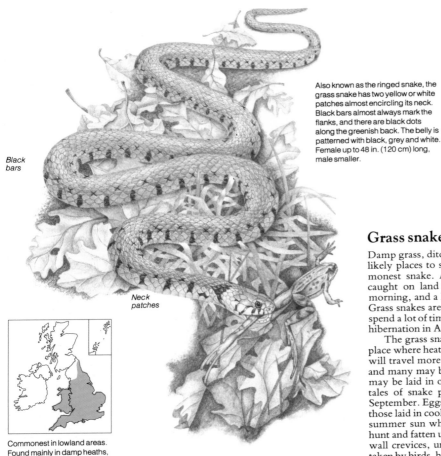

Also known as the ringed snake, the grass snake has two yellow or white patches almost encircling its neck. Black bars almost always mark the flanks, and there are black dots along the greenish back. The belly is patterned with black, grey and white. Female up to 48 in. (120 cm) long, male smaller.

Black bars

Neck patches

Commonest in lowland areas. Found mainly in damp heaths, woods, or in lush pastures.

Sites Guide

If it is threatened the grass snake may feign death, lying on its back with its tongue lolling out. It may also eject a foul-smelling fluid. Sometimes known as the water snake, the grass snake swims easily, diving under the water to escape detection and sometimes capturing its prey there. The grass snake may be seen at 1, 4, 8, 13, 14, 19–24, 29, 31.

Grass snake *Natrix natrix*

Damp grass, ditches, pond banks and slow-moving streams are likely places to see the grass snake, Britain's largest and commonest snake. Amphibians such as frogs are its main food, caught on land or in the water. It often feeds in the early morning, and a large meal will satisfy it for a week or ten days. Grass snakes are harmless to humans. Like other reptiles, they spend a lot of time basking in the spring sun after emerging from hibernation in April. Courting and mating follow soon after.

The grass snake is the only British snake to lay its eggs in a place where heat is generated, such as a compost heap. A female will travel more than a mile (up to 2 km) to find a suitable site, and many may be attracted to the same one. Hundreds of eggs may be laid in one manure heap in June or July, giving rise to tales of snake plagues when the young hatch in August or September. Eggs laid in hot places hatch some weeks earlier than those laid in cooler places, and the young have the benefit of the summer sun while growing, giving them plenty of energy to hunt and fatten up for winter. Hibernation begins in October, in wall crevices, under tree roots or in similar places. Snakes not taken by birds, hedgehogs or badgers may live about nine years.

Notes and Sketches

Dark back stripe

Male

Female

Dull brown is the typical lizard colouring, but it may be tinged red, yellow, grey or green. There is almost always a dark back stripe, and often dark side stripes with white edges. Stripes are sometimes broken. The female is fatter than the male and usually paler. About 6 in. (15 cm) long.

Widespread in open places throughout Britain. The only lizard in Scotland, Ireland.

A male's underside is usually orange with black spots, a female's lemon-yellow with no spots. Lizards have rows of scales across the underside, not single scales like snakes.

Female

Male

Common lizard *Lacerta vivipara*

Rustles in the undergrowth may be the first sign of a common lizard's presence as it scampers up a bank to hide. It is very nimble and disappears rapidly when disturbed. Lizards live in heathland, sand-dunes, grass or scrub-covered banks and on high moors, and where conditions are ideal large colonies may be found. They emerge from hibernation early in spring, and at first bask in the sun a good deal, but as the weather gets warmer they need to bask less. They court and mate in April and the young are born in midsummer. In the cool of September and October, lizards need to bask more often. Before autumn ends they retire into cracks and under stones to hibernate.

Common lizards eat a variety of small creatures, spiders particularly, which they hunt throughout warm days. At night and on cool days they remain hidden. Lizards themselves fall prey to many animals, including smooth snakes, adders, rats and birds – particularly kestrels. If a predator seizes a lizard's tail, it can shed it and so escape; the tail may even be shed if the lizard is merely threatened, to divert attention while it scuttles to safety. A new tail slowly grows from the stump, but is never as long or as perfect as the original.

Notes and Sketches

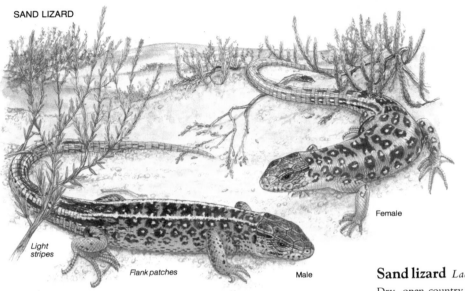

Light
stripes

Flank patches

Female

Male

SITES GUIDE

After mating, the female
sand lizard excavates a hole
in a sandy bank which is
sunny and warm and there
she lays her tiny oval eggs.
After hatching the lizards
have to grow quickly in order
to survive the rigours of
hibernation. Sand lizards are
now protected and no sites
are included in this book.

More heavily built and solidly marked
than the common lizard, the sand lizard
has two light stripes, sometimes
broken, along the back, with dark spots
between them. Black patches on the
flanks have pale centres. Males are
greenish, females brownish. About
7 in. (18 cm) long including tail.

In the north-west of England
prefers coastal dunes, but in
the south sandy heaths.

Young sand lizards can be
distinguished from common
lizards by their more
conspicuous spots.

Sand lizard *Lacerta agilis*

Dry, open country is the home of the sand lizard, chiefly the
sandy heaths of Surrey, Hampshire and Dorset, although a small
population lives on the coastal dunes near Liverpool. As the
heaths give way to farming and forestry and the sand-dunes
become less secluded, sand lizards have become scarce and are
declining still. Since 1975 they have been protected by law.

The sand lizard emerges from its hibernating burrow, dug
deep in the sand, in March or April, and spends some time
basking and shedding its old skin. Males normally emerge first,
their dull winter colours soon being replaced by emerald-green
flanks. In April and May the males fight fiercely for dominance,
the victors pairing up with females. Adult lizards feed well
during summer to build up fat reserves for the coming winter.
Large insects such as beetles and grasshoppers are the main food,
and they are often dismembered before being eaten. Sand lizards
may start hibernating as early as the end of August. Young
lizards are hatched in late August or September and grow
rapidly before they hibernate in October. Sand lizards need at
least two years to reach maturity. They may live to be seven or
eight if they escape the snakes, rats and birds that prey on them.

Notes and Sketches

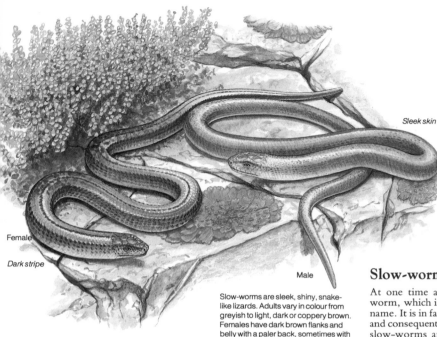

Sleek skin

Female

Dark stripe

Male

Slow-worms are sleek, shiny, snake-like lizards. Adults vary in colour from greyish to light, dark or coppery brown. Females have dark brown flanks and belly with a paler back, sometimes with a dark stripe. Males are more uniform in colour. Up to 18 in. (45 cm) long; just over half is tail.

SITES GUIDE

Like other lizards, if a slow-worm is captured by its tail, it is able to shed the end which continues to wriggle and writhe in a most convincing way, retaining the attention of its attacker while the reptile makes good its escape. Look out for slow-worms at 8, 11, 12, 15, 16, 19–22, 25, 27, 28, 31, 49, 50–52.

Widespread and common but shy and not often seen. Rarely basks in the open.

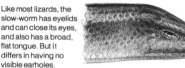

Like most lizards, the slow-worm has eyelids and can close its eyes, and also has a broad, flat tongue. But it differs in having no visible earholes.

Slow-worm *Anguis fragilis*

At one time any creeping, serpent-like animal was called a worm, which is how the slow-worm – or blind-worm – got its name. It is in fact a legless lizard but is often mistaken for a snake and consequently killed, although it is harmless. As slug-eaters, slow-worms are an asset to any garden. They usually move slowly and deliberately, but can move fast if disturbed.

Slow-worms live on sunny banks and hillsides where there is good cover such as grass, scrub or stones. Their shed skins, left in fragments, may be found occasionally. Hibernation underground begins in October and ends in March, when slow-worms emerge to bask in the early spring sun. Mating takes place in April and May. Males often fight at this time, seizing each other on or near the head and sometimes inflicting serious bites. From 6 to 12 young are born in August or September or, more rarely, in the following spring.

Young slow-worms have many predators, including frogs and toads. They take about three years to mature. Slow-worms can live longer than any other lizards, and one in captivity has reached its fifties. Such an age is unlikely in the wild, where enemies include hedgehogs, adders, rats and kestrels.

Notes and Sketches

Tracks and signs in downland and pasture

Most wild animals stay under cover during daylight hours, and venture out only after dark. As a result, few are likely to be seen in open fields and downland during the day. To the observant eye, however, there are usually plenty of signs that reveal the presence of quite a number of species. The signs described here are typical of the type of country shown, but are not the only ones that may be found there.

Because fields and grassland are frequently grazed by farm animals, the footprints, droppings and hairs of wild animals can easily be confused with those of domestic species. Sheep and deer, for instance, both have cloven hoofs, and it is very difficult to distinguish between their tracks. Generally, however, deer tracks in a particular spot are fewer in number than those of sheep, as sheep live in large groups. Deer are surprisingly common, even in heavily inhabited countryside, although they usually stay hidden from sight. Red, sika, fallow and roe deer are the species whose tracks are most likely to be confused with those of sheep. Pastureland where sheep graze is usually very close-cropped and unlikely to support many small mammals, except round field edges where hedgerows and longer grass afford food and shelter.

Rejected ragwort

A field with a lot of ragwort has probably been grazed by horses. Both horses and cows find ragwort distasteful but a horse can be more selective in its eating. It bites off plants between its teeth, whereas a cow pulls them up in clumps by curling its tongue round them.

A fox's leavings

The hind-leg bones and the foot of a rabbit are likely to be the remains of a fox's meal, and often have a distinctive, musky fox scent. They may have been dropped by a fox or, if the bones are picked clean, by a scavenging crow.

A fox's droppings

Fragments of bone, matted fur and seeds are contained in the droppings of a fox; the droppings have a very characteristic twisted tail.

Trampled trails in the grass

Beaten tracks in the grass that look like footpaths may be animal trails. If they pass under fences or low bushes and shrubs, they have been made by an animal. Footpaths made by humans go over or round such obstacles, or trample them down.

Sheep trails are usually narrow. They often cut deep into soft ground and expose the bare earth.

Badger paths are usually well-worn tracks about 6 in. (15 cm) wide. Normally the grass is flattened, but no earth is exposed.

Notes and Sketches

How to recognise hairs

Where animal trails pass under a chain-link or barbed-wire fence, hair can be scraped off an animal's back. Hairs caught on the top strand of a fence are likely to be from horses or cows, which rub their necks along it, or from deer that have leapt over it. Small deer also squeeze under fences.

Top wire

Cow hairs are fairly short and soft, and mat together like felt.

Deer hairs are stiff, straight and bristly.

Horses often catch long mane and tail hairs on barbed wire.

Badger hairs are wiry and 2–3 in. (50–75 mm) long. They are white, with a black zone near the tapered end.

Rabbit hairs are fine, soft and fluffy. They are about ½ in. (13 mm) long, and grey with a fawn tip.

Bottom wire

Fox hairs are about 1 in. (25 mm) long. They are straight and red-brown or grey-brown with a pale tip.

Where to look for footprints

A small patch of mud, often found near a gate or on a rutted path, is a good place to look for animal tracks. The cloven hoof-prints of sheep and deer are difficult to tell apart, but there may be other identifying signs near by, such as wool or hair.

Fore

Hind

A badger's fore and hind feet can be mistaken for the tracks of two different animals.

Tell-tale wisps

Where sheep have grazed, pieces of greyish-white fleece often get caught on brambles and thistles.

A dog's pawprints are broad and often have the front toes splayed.

A fox's tracks are narrow, with the front toes close together.

Sheep tracks have one half of the hoof larger than the other.

Deer tracks have both halves of the hoof the same size but often more widely separated.

Honey for the badger

Common wasps and some wild bees make nests underground in holes or burrows, often in a bank. A dug-up bees' nest is the work of a badger, which eats the larvae and stored honey. Its shaggy coat protects it from stings.

Notes and Sketches

Tracks and signs by the waterside

The muddy bank of a river or stream shows up animal footprints particularly well. So does the soft, moist soil of a water meadow – a riverside that in winter is deliberately flooded to keep the grass green and provide early grazing. The softer the mud, the finer the detail of the prints and the better the chance of very small prints showing up.

Animal footprints seen in the field are not always perfect specimens. Sometimes only the claws or toes may mark the soil, especially on dry ground, and there may be no print from the palm or sole of the foot. The fore feet of water voles and rats, for instance, often leave only sets of four small toe marks in an arc. Where several animals have crossed the ground, or one has moved repeatedly over the same area, there is likely to be a mass of confusing, overlapping prints. But there may be signs near by to give a clue to the animal's identity: food debris, for example, or a pile of droppings. As well as animals that live beside the water, look for the tracks of animals that come to drink at the water's edge, such as badgers, foxes and deer. Bird footprints, recognisable by the very long middle toe, are often numerous, particularly those of ducks, herons and moorhens.

Untidy voles

Chewed plant fragments, bitten-off stems and shreds of pith signify the presence of water voles, which feed on sedges and other waterside plants. Look out for tracks, droppings and also burrow entrances near by.

Cows may graze on waterside plants, but do not usually leave fragments lying about. Their cloven hoof prints, up to 3 in. (75 mm) long, are evident.

Water vole tracks are usually in groups, overlapping each other, around plant fragments. There may be wet, shiny patches where water has run off the fur.

Water vole droppings are oval and about ½ in. (13 mm) long. They are dark green or brown, usually in groups of about half a dozen, with vole prints all round them.

Footprints in focus

The soft, slimy mud at the water's edge shows very fine detail of even quite small footprints such as those of water voles, the ones most likely to be seen. They can be confused with the footprints of the brown rat, also seen near water. Mole footprints are occasionally seen in wet meadows, after flood water has forced them to leave their burrows.

Fore foot   Hind foot

A brown rat has four toes on its fore feet and five toes on its larger hind feet, but its prints are slightly larger than a water vole's. The rat's hind feet are 1⅓ in. (35 mm) long, or more.

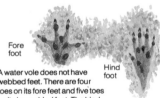

Fore foot

Hind foot

A water vole does not have webbed feet. There are four toes on its fore feet and five toes on its larger hind feet. The hind feet are up to 1 in. (25 mm) long.

Because a mole tends to walk on the inner side of its fore feet, its fore prints show only the marks of its five claw tips, not the rest of its foot. As its legs are short, its belly makes a drag mark in the mud.

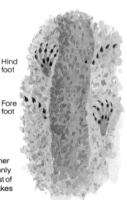

Hind foot

Fore foot

Geese among the mammals

Canada goose droppings – large, soft and green and white – are often seen in heaps beside water. Mammal droppings differ in having no white in them, nor are they as long and thin as the goose droppings.

Notes and Sketches

Burrows at the water's edge

Burrows may be found where there are low banks of soft earth by slow-flowing rivers. Water vole burrows and perhaps a kingfisher's nest-hole are the commonest.

A kingfisher's nest-hole is similar in size to a water vole burrow but is at least 24 in. (60 cm) above water level, and normally in a bare, vertical bank.

The entrance to a water vole burrow is a hole about 2 in. (50 mm) across. It is in a waterside bank at or near water level.

Territory markers

The droppings of aquatic mammals such as mink and otter may be found on a fallen tree or boulder at the water's edge. The animals leave the droppings as scent markers to define territory. Tracks in the mud near by help identification.

Mink droppings are smaller than otter spraints, but may also contain scales and bones. They are foul-smelling and when fresh are dark green.

Otter droppings (spraints) are dark and slimy with a strong, somewhat fishy smell. Fish scales and bone fragments may be visible.

Fore foot

Otter tracks show five-toed webbed feet. They are up to 2⅜ in. (60 mm) in length and about as wide as they are long. Drag marks made by the animal's tail can often be seen between the footprints.

Hind foot

Hind   Fore

Mink tracks show five-toed feet up to 1½ in. (40 mm) long. Web marks are not always visible. On the fore feet one toe is set back and close to the pad.

Notes and Sketches

An ever-ready larder

In mixed woods, squirrels often choose to live in conifers such as Scots pines, which provide them with year-round food and shelter. Look for chewed cones scattered beneath pines or other conifers.

A squirrel (red or grey) bites the scales off a ripe cone to get at the seeds inside. Chewed cores and neatly bitten-off scales are dropped.

Crossbills also drop discarded pine or spruce cones below trees. Usually the scales are not torn off but prised open with the beak and split.

Tracks in the mud

A muddy wheel rut in a woodland ride is a good place to look for animal tracks, particularly those of deer. Look, too, at the edge of a ditch where animals jump across.

Saplings spoiled by deer

In April roe bucks fray the bark of saplings such as birches when they rub off velvet from their new antlers. The ground below is churned up by their hooves. They also rub scent on saplings from April into July.

Red deer hoofprints are roughly 3¼ in. (83 mm) long and 2½ in. (64 mm) across.

Fallow deer hoofprints are roughly 2½ in. (64 mm) long and about 1½ in. (40 mm) across.

Hedgehog sign

Hedgehog droppings are sometimes seen on pathways. They are usually single, black, crinkly, about 1½ in. (40 mm) long and often studded with the remnants of chewed beetles.

Roe deer hoofprints are roughly 1⅜ in. (45 mm) long and 1⅜ in. (35 mm) across.

Dew claws

When deer jump and land in soft mud, their hoofprints are widely splayed and the dew claws are often imprinted.

Muntjac hoofprints are less than 1¼ in. (30 mm) long and 1 in. (25 mm) across.

Notes and Sketches

Tracks and signs in mixed woodland

Mixed woodland often provides shelter for more different kinds of animals than any other type of country, but it takes patience and a keen eye to find their signs. Tracks and trails do not show up well in leaf litter, and in autumn are soon hidden by falling leaves. But there are often animal footprints in the muddy rides and bare patches of soil, although it is rarely possible to follow a trail far before it becomes lost in the undergrowth. There are also animal signs such as hairs, droppings and food remains to be seen, although they are not easy to pick out amid the entanglement of trees and bushes.

On dry woodland soils, paw tracks – especially dog tracks – do not show the whole print, only the two front toes, and could be mistaken for the cloven hoofprints of deer. Usually the distinct claw marks to be seen at the tips of the toes of pawprints help to avoid confusion. The droppings of different species have distinctive shapes, but the colour and texture depend very much on what the animal has been eating, which often varies according to the time of year. Generally, groups of smooth, uniform pellets are those of plant eaters, and ragged pellets found singly or two or three together are those of carnivores.

Thickets that shelter deer

Deer often shelter beside a windproof holly thicket or dense coppice, or under yew trees. Piles of droppings (fewmets) accumulate there.

Fallow deer droppings are black and cylindrical with a small point at one end. They are roughly ⅝ in. (about 16 mm) long and usually in clusters.

Muntjac droppings are black and less than ½ in. (about 10 mm) long. They are round or slightly elongated and usually in clusters.

Red deer droppings are black and cylindrical with a small point at one end. They are up to 1 in. (25 mm) long and usually in clusters.

Roe deer droppings are oval and roughly ½ in. (10–15 mm) long. They are usually in clusters and may be black or brown.

Hazel tree harvest

Hazel nuts from woodland and hedgerow trees are a major food for rodents, which gnaw them in different ways depending on the species. Study the discarded remains of nuts to identify the eater. You may need a lens to see the toothmarks.

A bank vole gnaws a hole with a regular, clean-cut edge. It leaves few if any toothmarks on the nut surface.

A squirrel's jaws can shatter a nut in the same way as nutcrackers can. It leaves fragments of irregular shape with jagged edges and no obvious toothmarks.

A wood mouse gnaws a neat hole with an irregular, chamfered edge. There are traces of toothmarks on the nut's shiny surface.

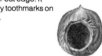

A dormouse gnaws a hole in the side of the nut and then enlarges it by turning the nut round and scooping the edge with its teeth. This leaves toothmarks on the cut edge but few on the nut surface.

Nests in coppice stools

Trees are coppiced by being cut off near the ground. This encourages the growth of clusters of slim, straight shoots for use as poles. Stumps (stools) accumulate a mass of dry, dead leaves that are ideal places for dormice to hibernate in winter. Several other species, such as wood mice, may nest there too.

Old bones for new

Antlers lying on the ground after being cast by deer are often gnawed by rodents, as they are a source of calcium, which helps to strengthen bones.

Notes and Sketches

Reading the stories in the snow

A layer of snow will show up the tracks of all kinds of animals not normally seen and whose presence was unsuspected. In snow, no animal can move anywhere without leaving its footprints, so snow provides an excellent opportunity to gain information about the movements and habits of wild creatures. Light snow, or even heavy frost, shows up individual tracks quite well. Thicker snow that blankets the ground often allows trails to be followed for considerable distances. In really deep snow, however, few trails are likely; it is so difficult to walk in that not many animals venture out.

Generally, only the tracks of fairly big animals – squirrels and larger creatures – are found in snow. Smaller animals such as mice and voles stay underneath the snow blanket because their food is there, and it is also warmer and more protected from icy winds. Trails in the snow often lead to where an animal has fed – where a rabbit has scraped through to find grass, for example. With the trail of a predator there may also be tracks of the prey, as well as its remains. Other signs of an animal, such as droppings or stains in the snow where it stopped to urinate, may also be found near its tracks.

Different ways of walking revealed

Trails in the snow usually have a whole succession of footprints, and so give a good opportunity to study the different ways in which animals walk.

A fox trail is almost a single line because a fox puts its hind feet into the prints of its fore feet and draws in its feet below the mid line of its body.

A dog trail has prints staggered to each side of its body line, being relatively wider-bodied and shorter-legged than a fox. It does not put its hind feet exactly into the prints of its fore feet.

A badger walks with its feet pointing inwards; the hind prints often overlap the rear of the fore prints. Often the prints are muddy from soil on the feet. Badgers do not hibernate; trails may be seen between sett entrances.

Hind foot Fore foot

How speed affects trails

The pattern of an animal's footprints varies according to its gait – hopping, trotting or galloping, for example.

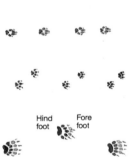

Hind foot (about 3½ in., 90 mm)

Fore foot

A rabbit moving slowly hops along. The prints of its hind feet are just behind the prints of its fore feet. But when it moves fast, it bounds in much longer strides. Its hind footprints appear in front of its fore footprints.

Hopping   Bounding

A trotting fallow deer places its hind feet just in front of the prints of its fore feet, producing a staggered trail of partly overlapping prints, all more or less evenly spaced. When galloping, it puts its hind feet well in front of its fore feet. Its prints are in fours, separated by longish gaps. Often prints are splayed and the marks of dew claws show.

Trotting   Galloping

Notes and Sketches

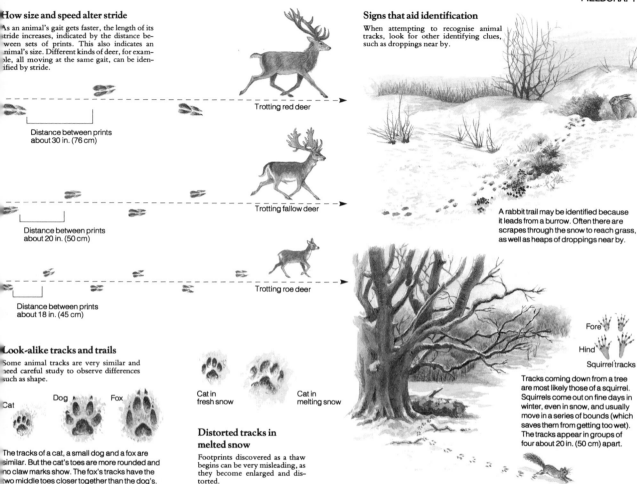

How size and speed alter stride

As an animal's gait gets faster, the length of its stride increases, indicated by the distance between sets of prints. This also indicates an animal's size. Different kinds of deer, for example, all moving at the same gait, can be identified by stride.

Trotting red deer

Distance between prints about 30 in. (76 cm)

Trotting fallow deer

Distance between prints about 20 in. (50 cm)

Trotting roe deer

Distance between prints about 18 in. (45 cm)

Look-alike tracks and trails

Some animal tracks are very similar and need careful study to observe differences such as shape.

Cat   Dog   Fox

The tracks of a cat, a small dog and a fox are similar. But the cat's toes are more rounded and no claw marks show. The fox's tracks have the two middle toes closer together than the dog's.

Cat in fresh snow   Cat in melting snow

Distorted tracks in melted snow

Footprints discovered as a thaw begins can be very misleading, as they become enlarged and distorted.

Signs that aid identification

When attempting to recognise animal tracks, look for other identifying clues, such as droppings near by.

A rabbit trail may be identified because it leads from a burrow. Often there are scrapes through the snow to reach grass, as well as heaps of droppings near by.

Fore

Hind

Squirrel tracks

Tracks coming down from a tree are most likely those of a squirrel. Squirrels come out on fine days in winter, even in snow, and usually move in a series of bounds (which saves them from getting too wet). The tracks appear in groups of four about 20 in. (50 cm) apart.

Notes and Sketches

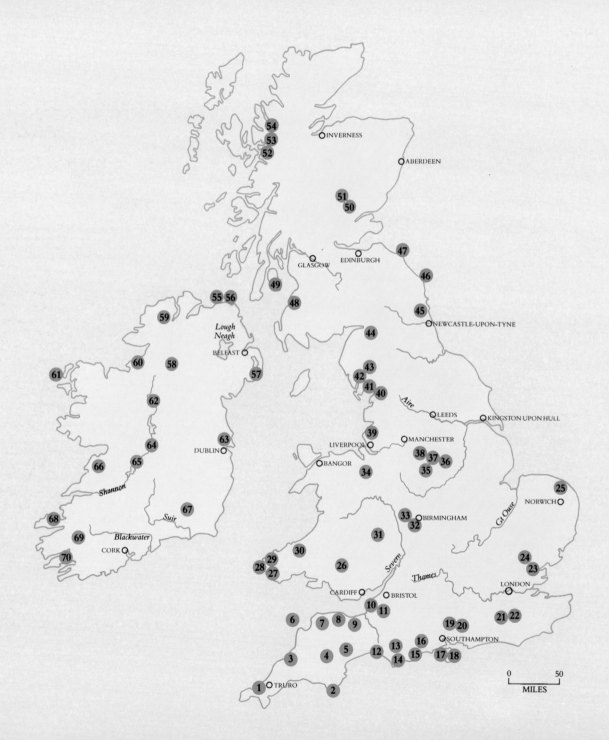

INVERNESS

ABERDEEN

54
53
52

51
50

47

46

EDINBURGH

GLASGOW

49

48

45

NEWCASTLE-UPON-TYNE

44

55 56

59

Lough Neagh

BELFAST

57

60

58

61

62

43
42
41
40

Aire

LEEDS

KINGSTON UPON HULL

64

DUBLIN

63

39

LIVERPOOL

MANCHESTER

BANGOR

34

38 37 36
35

66

65

Shannon

Suir

67

25

NORWICH

33

BIRMINGHAM

32

Gt Ouse

68

69

Blackwater

CORK

70

31

30

29

28 27

26

24

23

LONDON

Severn

Thames

CARDIFF

BRISTOL

10

11

6

7 8

9

19 20

21 22

16

SOUTHAMPTON

3

4

5

12

13

14

15

17 18

1 TRURO

2

0 _____ 50
MILES

The sites

This section comprises a gazetteer of sites in England, Wales, Scotland, Northern Ireland and the Republic of Ireland where you may see the species listed on pages 8–95. Sites in England, Wales and Northern Ireland are managed by the National Trust, those in Scotland by the National Trust for Scotland, and some of the sites managed by An Taisce are among those listed for the Republic of Ireland.

The order in which the sites are arranged on the following pages corresponds to the numbers on the map opposite. The gazetteer starts with the southernmost location in England and ends in the south-eastern corner of the Republic of Ireland. For ease of reference, there are three main sections: England and Wales, Scotland, and Ireland. Each section is preceded by an additional map, showing the sites relevant to that part of the country. So, if you are living or visiting the south of England, for example, you will be able to select those sites which are nearest your area.

The dots on the map are intended to give only a rough guide to each location. Each individual site entry will tell you which county the site is in and will give you more precise instructions on how to reach the property you wish to visit. Where applicable, opening times and admission fees are given and, of course, there is information on which species you may expect to see at the site.

Many of the places included in this book form part of the grounds of historic houses which are also open to the public. If you are interested in visiting the houses as well as their grounds and need further details of their opening times during the year and entry fees, check with your local tourist office.

English and Welsh sites

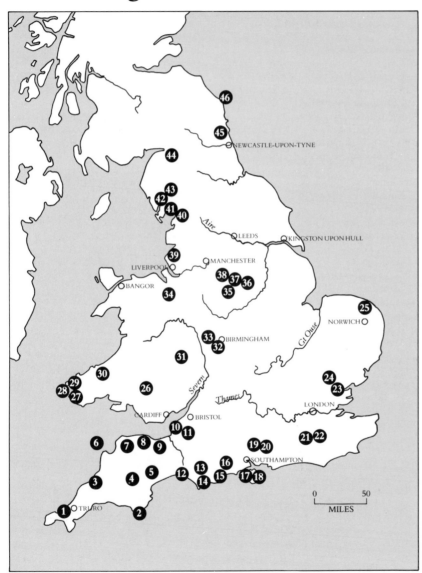

1 GODREVY TO PORTREATH

LOCATION *Cornwall*; **coast between headland 5 miles north-west of Camborne and village 6 miles north-west of Exeter, astride the B3301.**

This property not only lies within an Area of Outstanding Natural Beauty and contains part of a Site of Special Scientific Interest, it also has the long distance coastal path running through it. Lying on the north Cornish coast, it contains a variety of habitats including cliffs, dunes and coastal heath on the cliff tops with agricultural fields being cultivated inland.

Grey seals come to breed in the caves in the cliffs although the exact location of these is not precisely known. The Cornish 'hedges' of turfed stony banks surmounted by shrubby growth provide habitats for common lizards as well as small mammals such as wood mice. Stoats have been seen hunting here and the whole area must provide them with a useful hunting ground. Other animals which occur on this property are moles, grass snakes and rabbits. By their close and constant grazing, rabbits crop the grass as short as if it had been mown and prevent bramble and hawthorn scrub from growing.

2 SALCOMBE

LOCATION *Devon*; **6 miles of rugged cliffland between Bolt Tail and Overbeck, west of Salcombe.**

The 6 miles of scrub and heath-covered cliffs between Bolt Tail and Bolt Head to the west of the Kingsbridge Estuary, are all in the ownership of the National Trust. Cross the mouth of the harbour and 5 miles of similar habitat eastwards to Gammon Head also belong to the Trust. A number of streams have cut down through the cliffs on their way to the sea and the shelter supplied by these provides a habitat for scrub and tall vegetation. There are also woodlands on either side of the mouth of the estuary.

Here you can find two species of mammal, whose signs are easy to identify. Molehills are fairly common on the cliff tops and rabbit droppings and scrapings may also be frequently encountered. Foxes forage in this area, scavenging along the tide line or hunting for small mammals on the cliff tops. Look for the remains of an excavated rabbit 'stop' here. This is a dead-end burrow – often separate from the main warren – which is used as a breeding nest. A doe will have probably lined it with fur plucked from her chest.

Grey seals have been observed from the cliff tops and you may be lucky enough to see the dog-like head of a curious grey seal looking up from the water below. Common lizards have also been recorded on this property.

3 BOSCASTLE AND VALENCY VALLEY

LOCATION *Cornwall*; **5 miles north of Camelford. The valley runs for 2 miles along the river from Boscastle Harbour to the Church of St Juliet.**

Boscastle Harbour is a popular tourist resort lying on the north Cornish coast. The National Trust owns land along the cliffs on either side of the harbour including Penally Point and Forrabury Common and inland on the northern slopes of the Valency Valley. The best area for animals is Peters Wood where the main tree species is oak together with a scattering of ash and sycamore. Its natural history interest is reflected by the fact that it is leased to the Cornwall Trust for Nature Conservation.

Dormice live in the wood and you may spot their nests – made of dry leaves, moss, grass and bark from plants like honeysuckle – among bramble. Winter is the best time to search for these, although the dormice themselves should be hibernating underground elsewhere in the wood and will not be using their nests then.

Peters Wood is also noted for its roosts of bats, many species of which are now considered rare. Daubenton's and long-eared have been recorded here in the past.

Moving out to the coast, the more isolated coves are sometimes chosen by grey seals who haul out to breed and moult. Look out, too, for badger, fox, mink, weasel, grey squirrel, harvest mouse, wood mouse, bank vole and mole.

4 CASTLE DROGO

LOCATION *Drewsteignton, Devon*; **1 mile south-west of Drewsteignton. OPEN Apr to end Oct: daily 11–6. ADMISSION Garden and grounds £1.20.**

Castle Drogo lies within the Dartmoor National Park and is on the north-eastern edge of the moor. The estate is bisected by the River Teign which runs through a deep wooded gorge overlooked by the castle on a rocky outcrop.

The major woodland areas of Whiddon and Drewston Woods consist largely of oak coppice with a uniform structure and poor shrub layer. Foxes are known to live here and you may see their droppings which are generally deposited in prominent locations – on rocks and molehills, for example. Fox droppings are recognisable because they taper to a 'tail' and sometimes turn white as they get older.

Other rewarding sites where you should find animals are the damp areas alongside the river. Grass snakes are known to occur here and the soft-footed observer may be able to approach these reptiles as they bask in the sunshine. You may also see common lizard, rabbit, water vole, wood mouse, bank vole, field vole, grey squirrel and fallow deer.

5 KILLERTON

LOCATION *Devon*; **7 miles north-east of Exeter, astride the B3181. OPEN Garden and park open all day during daylight hours. ADMISSION Garden £1.50. Winter rate 50p.**

Killerton is located beside the M5 beyond Exeter to the north-east. Although much of it is under agricultural management, there is a substantial woodland at Ashclyst Forest which, although it is largely a secondary wood, does contain sections of old oak woodland. The tree species are very mixed and, in addition to oak, include sweet chestnut, sycamore, beech, birch and evergreen oak.

Look for signs of badger here and for the diggings and droppings of rabbits. Of major importance in this area, though, is the large population of roe deer. Their tracks and signs are very evident although only the quiet or the fortunate will see the animals themselves. Grey squirrels may also be seen and heard in the woods. Other species to look out for are mole, pygmy shrew, fox and common lizard.

6   LUNDY

LOCATION *Devon*; **seal island in the Bristol Channel, 11 miles north of Hartland Point.**
OPEN All year.
ADMISSION £2.

The area around this granite island, which measures 3 miles by 1 mile and which rises to over 400 feet above the sea, is going to be declared a Marine Nature Reserve. The now disused old light was located at one of the highest points on Lundy but had to be abandoned in favour of two lower lighthouses, one at either end, because it was too often shrouded in fog. The majority of the island is covered with rough grassland which is grazed by the island's herd of sika deer, rabbits, a flock of Soay sheep and feral goats as well as domestic cattle, and most of these species can be seen fairly easily.

However, Lundy is best known for its grey seals. It has a small population of probably no more than 120 individuals and they may be seen all around the island, hauled out on suitable rocks. They do have favourite places such as Seal's Rock, Surf Point and Shutter Point, but at the slightest sign of danger they will take to the water. Here they may dive out of sight for up to 20 minutes but are more likely to hang in the water, 'bottling' with only their heads sticking out of the water, until the danger has passed.

The top of the grey seal's head is flat so it can be distinguished from the common seal which is smaller and which has a round head. Grey seals eat larger fish than common seals – their diet includes cod, whiting and salmon – and they will even raid fishing nets to take them. Both on land and in water, grey seals are often very noisy, barking, moaning, hooting, hissing and snarling. You may hear a seal before you can see it.

7   ARLINGTON COURT

LOCATION *Devon*; **7 miles north-east of Barnstaple on the A39.**
OPEN Garden and park open all year during daylight hours.

This large estate lies to the west of Exmoor in hilly countryside with deep wooded valleys. The River Yeo runs through the property and is surrounded by mature oak and beech woodland, some of which is coppiced, together with plantations and young softwoods. All of the woods are used by red deer although the oak woods are clearly preferred and the tracks and signs left by the deer are most obvious in these.

The best places to look for deer are north and south of Tuckers Bridge where old riverside meadows have been abandoned in the past and have been invaded from the woodlands. The deer come to drink and to wallow in the river in the summer and autumn and to graze in the winter. Foxes have also been recorded at Arlington Court.

8   HOLNICOTE

LOCATION *Somerset*; **estate covering 4½ miles of coastline between Porlock Bay and Minehead and extending 6 miles south from the north coast.**

This huge estate of almost 12,500 acres lies in the north-east corner of Exmoor. It includes a continuous area of moorland stretching from Almsworthy Common in the west to Brockwell in the east and encompassing Dunkery Beacon, the highest point on Exmoor. Other moorland areas take in Ley Hill, Bossington Hill and Selworthy Beacon. On the steep valley sides of Horner Water is one of the largest blocks of semi-natural woodland in England.

The moorland areas consist largely of an undulating plateau dissected by steepsided combes. The predominant vegetation is dwarf shrub heath – mainly heather, sometimes mixed with bilberry and gorse. Wet heath also occurs and the combes and valley sides generally grow a mixture of bracken and gorse. The most significant mammal here is the red deer and the herd on this estate is estimated at 200 individuals. It is believed that they were introduced from parkland stock and do not form part of the pure British race now confined to Scotland and the north of England.

The estate runs out to the sea on the north coast of Somerset where there are sandy beaches and cliffs. Grey seals have been recorded here but are not known to breed. You may also see common lizard, slow-worm, grass snake, adder, common frog, common toad, roe deer, fox, badger, mink, grey squirrel, brown hare, rabbit, hedgehog, mole, dormouse, harvest mouse and wood mouse.

The wood mouse feels just as much at home in sand dunes as in woodland. Males will regularly forage over a territory roughly half the size of a football pitch, which might seem enormous for such a small animal. Perhaps suprisingly, wood mice have large hind feet that enable them to leap away like kangaroos. They usually move very fast, often bounding with their front feet tucked up. The mice also climb well and will often use somewhere high as a feeding place.

9 THE QUANTOCKS

LOCATION *Somerset*; a ridge of hills running north-west to south-east, extending from Quantoxhead to Kingston.

The National Trust's landholding in the Quantocks amounts to nearly 1,000 acres covering a number of properties. The whole falls within the Quantocks Area of Outstanding Natural Beauty. There are areas of sessile oak woodland at Willoughby Cleeve and Shervage Wood while much of the remainder is heath and grass-heath. While the majority of the oak woodland is on average 70 to 100 years old, there are a few older trees of around 150 years of age in Willoughby Cleeve. Shervage Wood, on the other hand, is an old coppiced oak woodland whose trees have spreading branches. Neither wood has a good shrub layer although holly, hazel and bramble do occur.

Grey squirrels are known to live in both woods and their feeding signs may be seen. Look for stumps and stones with old nut shells on, which the squirrels have used as look-out points while eating. You may also see the animals themselves, or hear their churring calls of annoyance. Both red deer and fox have been noted in Shervage Wood and their footprints and droppings are apparent in places. Fox droppings are left on a high point such as an ant hill, molehill or stone. They generally have a wispy 'tail' and sometimes turn white as they age because of their high calcium content.

Adders and common lizards inhabit the areas of heath and grass-heath, basking in the sun but rarely far from cover into which they disappear at the slightest disturbance. Other species to look out for are common frog, mole and rabbit.

10 BREAN DOWN

LOCATION *Somerset*; the south arm of Weston Bay, 2 miles south-west of Weston-super-Mare.

Brean Down looks very much like an island when viewed at a distance from Weston-super-Mare while even at close quarters its links with the rest of Somerset are tenuous. The Down itself is a long block of limestone rising 250 feet above the sea and almost as much above the flat 'levels' to which it is joined. Steps lead up the steep south side to allow visitors to climb to its summit. There are excellent views from here, inland to the Mendips and Brent Knoll and out to sea across to Wales with the islands of Steep Holm and Flat Holm standing in the Bristol Channel.

Brean Down is covered mainly with bracken and bramble scrub, which provides ideal cover for a number of mammals. Rabbits do well here, enjoying the calcareous grasses on the cliff edges and burrowing easily into the light shallow soil. Look for their spherical droppings on high points such as ant hills. You may also discover a shallow hole dug out with nesting material – dried vegetation and rabbit fur – outside. This is the remains of a rabbit's nest or 'stop' which has been excavated by a fox to reach the baby rabbits inside.

You may also see the black cigar-shaped droppings of hedgehogs which live here, together with moles and stoats. Male and female stoats look alike, but a fully grown male can be up to 50 per cent bigger than a female. Pairs may be seen together briefly in summer, at breeding time. Once a year, there is a litter of six or more young. They first leave the den at about five weeks old and often hunt and play in a family group.

11 CHEDDAR CLIFFS

LOCATION *Somerset*; 8 miles north-west of Wells.

The dramatic gorge at Cheddar, with its soaring grey limestone cliffs, tends to draw attention away from the large areas of mixed woodland and open grassland on either side of the road here. The National Trust owns most of the northern side of the gorge where there are woods of ash and hazel with a scattering of whitebeam and yew, sycamore and larch.

Two unusual small mammals are to be found – the common dormouse and the yellow-necked mouse. Both species are nocturnal and very secretive so you are most unlikely to see them. The dormouse spends most of its waking hours at night feeding in the tree canopy, except when it is in winter hibernation, while the yellow-necked mouse is also surprisingly arboreal. Fortunately both are fond of hazelnuts and, as the teeth marks they leave on the empty nut shells are characteristically different, the observant nature detective can search for such shells and discover if these mammals are present.

Being limestone, the gorge has a large number of caves many of which are used by bats for summer roosts. The caves also provide sheltered, humid places in which bats can hibernate during winter. Some of the caves are closed with grilles to protect bats, which are now an endangered species.

Badgers are common in this area and their well trodden paths are clearly visible. Look out for muddy marks and scratches on the stones of walls where these animals have climbed over on their nightly forays. Also here are slow-worm, common lizard, adder, brown hare, rabbit, grey squirrel, stoat and mole.

12   GOLDEN CAP

LOCATION *Dorset*; **4 miles east of Lyme Regis across Lyme Bay; about 3 miles south-west of Bridport. Access via A35 from Morcombelake and Chideock. The estate contains 15 miles of footpath.**

This large and complex estate falls within the West Dorset Heritage Coast area. The immediate seaboard, with its well-known undercliffs, has also been designated a Site of Special Scientific Interest by the Nature Conservancy Council.

These undercliffs are mainly inaccessible and only rabbits, hares and roe deer graze here, for farm stock are largely excluded. Badgers, too, seem to favour the undercliff area, probably because it is quiet and undisturbed. Much of the undercliff is overgrown with scrub and coarse grassland enabling roe deer to lie up in safety. Slow-worms have also been recorded here sunbathing during the day and emerging at night to hunt. Other animals observed at Golden Cap include fox, mole and palmate newt.

13   RINGMOOR

LOCATION *Dorset*; **downland site north of Turnworth, 4 miles west of Blandford Forum.**

This is a very small but interesting and little disturbed property nestling in the downs. A mosaic of different habitats may be found here including open grassland invaded in parts by scrub, hazel coppice, oak, ash and hazel woodland and two ponds. The oak woodland has a high canopy, beneath which is a lower one of sycamore and a shrub layer of hawthorn, holly, hazel and elder.

A number of large horizontal trunks are used extensively by squirrels as feeding tables and you may see the discarded scales and cores of larch cones. If you are careful and quiet, you may also see roe deer. They are cautious deer and very alert but it is possible to move stealthily through the undergrowth and spot them feeding. They sometimes lie up in patches of vegetation that look impossibly small, often hiding among brambles, tall grasses and nettles for this purpose.

You may also see signs of mole, rabbit, badger and grass snake.

14   SOUTHDOWN FARM

LOCATION *Dorset*; **7 miles south-east of Dorchester and 5 miles east of Weymouth on Ringstead Bay.**

This property is designated for both its outstanding beauty and its scientific interest. It is crossed by the long distance Dorset Coastal Path. The Southdown Farm section of the property runs inland for almost a mile and, although this is agricultural land with much of it under cultivation, it does include some areas of willow scrub and good hedgerows. The coastal strip of cliffs and undercliffs consists of a mosaic of habitats. Scrub is common, along with more open chalk grassland and coarse grassland.

As a result of the Dorset Trust for Nature Conservation's work, the records for the animals here are extensive. Adders are common, especially in the coarse grassland and scrub areas and a number of their prey species – common lizard, bank vole, pygmy shrew and wood mouse – have also been observed. Stoats and weasels, too, are known to hunt in the area and will make good use of hedgerows for cover and as corridors to travel from one hunting ground to another. Badgers have been seen on the property and you may discover their paths and possibly their territorial dung pits.

You should also look for smooth newt, grass snake, rabbit, fox, hare, mole and grey squirrel.

15   BROWNSEA ISLAND

LOCATION *Dorset*; **reached by ferry from Poole Quay and Sandbanks. Visitors may land their own boats at the Pottery Pier at the west end of the island.**
OPEN **28 Mar to 27 Sept; daily 10–8 or dusk if earlier.**
ADMISSION **Landing fee £1; parties 70p by written arrangement with the Warden.**

Brownsea Island is 500 acres in extent and stands in the waters of Poole Harbour. Much of it is wooded with a mixture of oak, beech, sweet chestnut and Scots pine and an understorey which ranges from the sparse, through bracken and bramble to the dense cover of rhododendron.

Even though it is an island, Brownsea provides a suitable habitat for a surprisingly long list of animals. Of these, the most famous are probably the red squirrels which rely on the island's isolation to separate them from their grey counterparts. The red squirrel watcher should move quietly through the woods, pausing frequently to listen and look around. The squirrels are most likely to be feeding in the canopy and may be spotted taking pine cones and other fruits or heard as they discard the inedible parts which tumble down through the twigs and leaves.

Sika deer also live on the island and spend much of their time lying up in cover. They may be seen early or late in the day but you are more likely to find their wine-bottle shaped droppings or their tracks in damp ground. Seven species of bat have been recorded on Brownsea and·they roost either in hollow trees or in buildings. Although you cannot see the roosts themselves, you may find bat droppings adhering to the walls below the entrances.

Look out too, for common lizard, slow-worm, hedgehog, common shrew, pygmy shrew, rabbit, water vole, wood mouse, harvest mouse, black rat, brown rat, stoat, weasel, mink and roe deer.

16   PEPPERBOX HILL

LOCATION *Wiltshire*; 5 miles south-east of Salisbury, on the north side of the A36.

There are wonderful views of the surrounding countryside from the top of Pepperbox Hill, which is a small National Trust property containing a mosaic of habitats. The major ones are dense scrub with a population of juniper, rough grassland and arable fields, together with two outlying areas of beech woodland.

The animal records for this site are good and include a number of small mammals. One of these is the harvest mouse and you may find its nests in the long grasses. Search in the autumn in grass tussocks for neatly woven nests. This open downland countryside is good habitat for brown hares, and the observant watcher may see the still form of a hare sitting quietly in the

middle of a field. Alternatively, a frightened animal may be spotted as it runs away from danger at high speed.

Other animals which may be seen include mole, field vole, bank vole, wood mouse, grey squirrel, rabbit, fox, badger, stoat, weasel, roe deer and slow-worm.

17   NEWTOWN

LOCATION *Isle of Wight*; 5 miles west of Newport, 1 mile north of the A3054.

This is a varied property which includes extensive areas of estuarine habitat. There are about 88 acres of woodland, most of it included in Walter's Copse and Town Copse which lead down to Clamerkin Creek, part of the Newtown River estuary. Much of the property falls within the Newtown Local Nature Reserve and is a designated Site of Special Scientific Interest.

Both of the above copses are a mixture of oak and hazel and Walter's Copse also contains ash and field maple. The Isle of Wight as a whole is known for its population of red squirrels which survive here without incursions from the greys. Their population density is not as great as that of grey squirrels and they are more arboreal, spending much less time on the ground. This will tend to make them more elusive and difficult to see. Nevertheless, the quiet and careful naturalist should be able to spot red squirrels here. Dormice, too, live in this wood and it is worth searching the ground for the telltale shells of hazelnuts, especially in the late summer.

Various species of bat are to be found in this area and noctule, brown long-eared, whiskered and serotine have all been observed. The roost of noctules in hollow

trees may be identified by the dark moist streak beneath the entrance hole.

You should also look for adder, common lizard, rabbit, fox and mole.

18   BORTHWOOD COPSE

LOCATION *Isle of Wight*; 2 miles west of Sandown, just north of the A3056.

Borthwood Copse is a small woodland – almost all that remains of a once extensive medieval hunting forest. It lies inland of Sandown and Shanklin, within an Area of Outstanding Natural Beauty. The main tree species is oak; some of these are in a form known as 'standards' and are large trees 45 feet to 60 feet tall which have been allowed to grow to maturity. Among and below them are coppiced oaks, with between four and eight stems growing from a single rootstock or 'stool'. In the past, these would have been cropped from time to time for their timber, the stool then growing stems anew. There is also hazel coppice in this wood together with a number of horse chestnut trees mixed with pine – an ideal habitat for squirrels.

The Isle of Wight is acknowledged as being one of the few places left in southern England where red squirrels are abundant and you may see them here. Look out, too, for holes in some of the larger sweet chestnut trunks. These may indicate a hollow tree used as a roost by bats, usually noctules. A grey-brown stain below the hole is a good indicator of such use. You will find a pair of binoculars handy when checking trees for such signs. Moles, wood mice and bank voles also live in the copses, and you should find signs of their presence even if you do not see them. They have all been observed at Borthwood Copse.

19   SELBORNE HILL

LOCATION *Hampshire*; 4 miles south
of Alton, between Selborne and New-
ton Valence, west of the B3006.

Selborne has been well known among
naturalists for two centuries following the writings of Gilbert White. Its
wildlife importance is recognised today
through the designation of the majority of
the property as a Site of Special Scientific
Interest. Most of the property is
woodland, one of the main features of
which is the very steep north-facing scarp
slope, with beech 'hangers'. While the
canopy trees are largely pure beech or
beech mixed with oak and ash, the species
in the understorey are very varied and
include a good quantity of hazel particularly on the lower 'hanger' slopes.

Dormice have been reported here and
in the gardens adjacent to The Scrubs
where hibernating individuals may be
discovered during winter and early spring
gardening tasks. Look out for characteristically gnawed nut shells. Badgers also live
in the area.

Wood Pond on the edge of the grassland clearing contains both smooth and
palmate newts and grass snakes have been
observed hunting near the pond. Inter-
estingly, the damp and dry habitats
favoured respectively by the grass snake
and the adder often occur in close prox-
imity as they do here. Early spring mornings are a good time to see adders sunbathing. They do this to raise their body
temperatures to a heat at which their
muscles, senses and digestion are fully
active.

Look out, too, for slow-worm, fox,
grey squirrel, mole and roe deer, all of
which have been sighted and recorded on
this property in the past.

20 PASSFIELD COMMON AND CONFORD MOOR

LOCATION *Hampshire*; 2 miles north-
west of Liphook.

Parts of Passfield Common are sup-
posedly relics of the old Woolmer
Forest and ancient woodland species of
lichen are found here. Mostly, however,
the biological interest in this property lies
in the areas of fen, wet heath and dry
heath. Indeed, Conford Moor Site of
Special Scientific Interest has been so
designated because of its wetland communities.

Of the 231 acres of this property, 150
acres are woodland and woodland scrub.
Ash, oak and alder occur and roe deer lie
up in their cover during the day. The fen
areas consist mainly of Conford Bog and
adjacent carr areas (alder copses), together
with Hollywater Pond, and these provide
good habitats for amphibians and reptiles.
In particular, grass snakes have been noted
here, while slow-worms and other reptiles
may be found in the bracken areas.

There may also be opportunities to see
moles, grey squirrels, rabbits, foxes,
adders, common lizards and toads.

21   BOX HILL

LOCATION *Surrey*; 1 mile north of
Dorking, 2½ miles south of Leather-
head, east of the A24, close to Burford
Bridge.
OPEN All Year. Pay and Display car/
coach parks at top of hill.

The River Mole cuts through the
North Downs immediately to the
west of Box Hill. The deep and steep-
sided valley it has carved here accentuates
the bulk of Box Hill which is especially
prominent. Its south-facing slope is particularly steep. The Mole Gap, as it is
known, has been designated a Geological
Conservation Review Site.

Box Hill is well known for its areas of
chalk grassland and also for its profuse
growth of box, which occurs as a shrub
layer in the property's extensive
woodland. It is here that most of the
animals are to be found. Very little ancient
woodland survives at Box Hill and most
has been planted or has regenerated. On
the steep slopes, beech-dominated woods
are most common together with a mixture of yew, oak, hazel, box and ash, while
on the plateau, beech and oak are the
major species with areas of hazel coppice
along with box and other species.

You should search here for nutshells
opened by bank vole, dormouse, yellow-
necked mouse and grey squirrel. Look out
too for tracks of deer and fox and the trails
of badgers. The silent and diligent watcher
may even see a stoat or a weasel. Stoats can
move very fast, perhaps up to 20 miles an
hour in bounds of about 20 inches.
Usually they will try to keep to the cover
of hedges, walls and fences. Prey is unlikely to escape either a stoat or a weasel once
it is in pursuit – both animals kill their
victim with a bite at the back of the neck.
Stoats will tackle prey larger than themselves, but weasels tend to hunt smaller
animals. Voles and mice are their main
food, though occasionally they will try for
small birds, rats and rabbits.

The following species have also been
recorded at Box Hill: common lizard,
slow-worm, grass snake, rabbit, grey
squirrel, roe deer, mole, fox, weasel,
fallow deer, badger, stoat, bank vole,
common shrew, field vole, pygmy shrew,
wood mouse, yellow-necked mouse,
water vole, water shrew and dormouse.

22 LIMPSFIELD COMMON

LOCATION *Surrey*; **south-east of Oxted, extending to the county boundary.**

This is a typical Surrey common with areas of ancient beech and oak and secondary woodland of oak, birch and sycamore with pine plantations. In parts there are coppiced oaks with some elderly standards and, in places, Scots pine dominates. Beyond the woods are areas of acid grassland and a few patches of heather. Part of the eastern section falls into the Limpsfield Chart and Cronklands Site of Special Scientific Interest.

It appears to be a good area for reptiles, especially around the golf course and where the common is more open. Here, particularly in the spring, you may see adders basking in the sun, their bodies flattened to absorb as much heat as possible. Lizards, too, take full advantage of any slight bank or rise which will both give them shelter and tilt their recumbent bodies towards the sun.

Other species recorded here include rabbit, fox, grey squirrel, roe deer, badger, grass snake and slow-worm. You are unlikely to see a slow-worm out in the open – they prefer to bask in partial sunlight, not in the direct glare of the sun's rays, where they are less visible to predators. They sometimes drape themselves among the twigs of old heather or lie under thin stone slabs – or under corrugated iron, if they can find any. Much of the slow-worm's time is spent underground and you might find a slow-worm in an ants' nest though they do not seem to eat ants very often.

Slugs are the slow-worm's favourite food. It seizes one by the middle and then swallows it whole. Insects, spiders and other small creatures are also eaten. The slow-worm will only take live prey – never carrion. If a slow-worm itself is seized, by a hungry bird, for example, it will escape by shedding its tail. The stump will eventually heal, but the tail will never grow back to its original length.

23 BLAKE'S WOOD

LOCATION *Essex*; **about 5 miles east of Chelmsford, just south-west of Little Baddow.**

Blake's wood is a National Trust property which is managed as a nature reserve by the Essex Naturalists' Trust and which forms part of a Site of Special Scientific Interest designated by the Nature Conservancy Council. It is a mixed hardwood woodland. Large old oaks grow here among coppiced sweet chestnuts while ash, birch, field maple and hornbeam are also found. Several streams run through these woods and alders line some of their banks. There are pools and wet areas too, and these attract both common toads and grass snakes.

A good record has been kept of the small mammal population. Wood mice and yellow-necked mice have both been noted. The latter is the larger animal with a complete collar of brown fur. It is more arboreal than the wood mouse and frequently climbs high into trees in search of food. Dormice are also known to occur in Blake's Wood. In the past they have been found breeding in nest boxes put up for birds. You may find hazelnut shells opened by any of these three animals. Look for them on the ground especially in the early autumn when they are first ripe. You many also find signs of rabbit, pipistrelle bat, fox and badger here.

24 HATFIELD FOREST

LOCATION *Essex*; **3 miles east of Bishop's Stortford on the south side of the A120.**

This country park is remarkable in that medieval woodland management is being continued today. There are areas of traditional 'coppice with standards' woodland, where ash, hazel, hornbeam and maple are still used for coppicing and are cut every 16 years in rotation. This harvest is used for hurdles, wall wattles, thatching spars and firewood. 'Standard' trees are allowed to grow on to become mature, providing larger timber, originally used for ships and houses. There are also open greens where the standard trees are still pollarded, which is another form of management. Hatfield Forest was acquired by the National Trust in 1924 and has since been designated both a Country Park and a Site of Special Scientific Interest. The property includes a lake and areas of scrub and open grassland as well as the coppices and old pollard trees.

Once red deer used this area but the last of these was killed during the First World War. Fallow deer, escapees from deer parks elsewhere, find shelter here. These deer do become accustomed to people and one way of getting close to them is to walk past the deer to a position down wind, in the company of a chattering group and, while your friends continue on their way, stalk quietly back to the deer. Muntjac are also known to use the park and you may see their tiny slots or footprints in soft ground. These tiny deer spend much of their time in shrubby undergrowth and their pathways are clearly visible.

You may also see mole, rabbit, toad, grey squirrel, dormouse, badger, fox, grass snake and common frog.

25   BLICKLING HALL

LOCATION *Norfolk*; 1½ miles north-west of Aylsham, 15 miles north of Norwich, 10 miles south of Cromer on the north side of the B1354.
OPEN 11 Apr to 1 Nov: daily except Mon and Thur but open Bank Hol Mon 1–5; closed Good Fri.
ADMISSION Garden £1.50; house £2.50; pre-booked parties £2.00.

The National Trust estate at Blickling extends to almost 5,000 acres although much is intensively farmed and of little biological interest. There are, however, a number of very good habitats including a length of the River Bure which passes through the estate, unimproved riverside pastures and their accompanying drains or ditches, a lake and a section of disused railway.

Mink have been noted along the river. These dark, cat-sized mustelids may be seen hunting prey such as rabbits and moorhens during the day, or you might come across their black and rather smelly droppings at strategic points. You can distinguish a swimming mink from a swimming otter by its more pointed snout, darker colouring and smaller size. It has a longer body and thicker tail than a water vole. Mink swim well, often catching some of their food in the water.

The disused railway line is a favourite place for slow-worms which enjoy basking on the sunny side of the railway cutting. Rabbits also inhabit these areas, making full use of the disturbed ground, or man-made features such as culverts, to conceal themselves from predators.

You may also see hedgehog, mole, Daubenton's bat, noctule bat, pipistrelle bat, hare, wood mouse, water vole, brown rat, grey squirrel, stoat, weasel and fox.

26   BRECON BEACONS

LOCATION *Powys*; mountain range to south and south-west of Brecon.

More than 9,000 acres of the Brecon Beacons are owned by the National Trust. All this land lies within the Brecon Beacons National Park and much of it is included in the Pen y fan Site of Special Scientific Interest designated by the Nature Conservancy Council. The Trust ownership includes Pen y fan, which is the highest point on the Beacons at nearly 3,000 feet in height.

There is a steep scarp face to the north, into which a series of corries and crags have been cut, while the southern slope is much more gentle and sweeping. Most of the upland is grazed hill-land, supporting a grassland and grass-heath vegetation. Foxes live up here and grey squirrels have also been recorded, straying far from the trees below.

For those interested in amphibians, the corrie lake known as Llyn-cwm-llwch is where you will find palmate newts, recorded as being abundant here, together with frog tadpoles at the right time of the year.

Other species recorded in the Brecon Beacons include common lizard, polecat, mink, hare, pipistrelle bat, wood mouse, yellow-necked mouse and mole.

27   MARLOES, ST BRIDE'S BAY

LOCATION *Dyfed*; 7 miles west of Milford Haven, at the south end of St Bride's Bay.

The National Trust property at Marloes encompasses the whole of the headland and incorporates a considerable amount of coastline. Some of this estate falls within a Site of Special Scientific Interest and part is within Skomer Marine Reserve. The whole area is in the Pembrokeshire Coast National Park and the coast path passes through.

The great variety of habitat includes scrub and coarse and maritime grassland along the cliff top, while inland there is agricultural land some of which surrounds Marloes Mere. This is a wetland area, let in part to the West Wales Trust for Nature Conservation.

The scrub and grasses of the cliff top and cliff edge contain a small mammal population composed largely of bank voles and wood mice although field voles also occur. These, in turn, provide food for a range of predators. The small mustelids are represented by the weasel and stoat, although the latter may also take rabbits which are present too. Both fox and badger live here and the fox especially will capture many voles.

The Marloes Mere area contains a good selection of amphibians and you should look out for frogs, toads and palmate newts. Other species to watch for on this property are common lizard, adder, slow-worm, hedgehog, mole, shrew, pipistrelle bat, house mouse and grey squirrel.

28   ST BRIDE'S BAY

LOCATION *Dyfed*; west-facing bay stretching from Ramsey Sound in the north to Skomer in the south and to Rickets Head in the east.

Extensive lengths of the west Welsh coastline within the Pembrokeshire Coast National Park – including blocks around St David's Head to the north of St Bride's Bay – are owned by the National

Trust. The habitats are very mixed here and range from scrub woodland to maritime grassland, cliffs and foreshore.

Blackthorn-dominated scrub occurs in a number of locations including Solva and Porth-clais inlets, at Pointz Castle and the Caerbwdy Valley. This vegetation mix provides ideal cover for both foxes and badgers and signs of both species are apparent in the area. They scavenge on the beach as well as capturing small mammals, earthworms and beetles among the grasses of the cliff tops.

Of special note in this area is the presence of grey seals. They come to the Pembrokeshire coast to breed in the sea caves and the observant visitor should see them in reasonable numbers here at various times of the year. Look out, too, for common frog, adder, common lizard, slow-worm, rabbit, mole and field vole.

29 ST DAVID'S COMMONS

LOCATION *Dyfed*; over 50 areas of common land lying between St David's Head and Fishguard.

The St David's peninsula is scattered with a variety of commons. They cover a range of habitats but fall into a number of general categories. Streams run through many, or even rise from springs on the commons themselves. Others are situated on rocky knolls while two, Sickly Common and Ciliau Moor, include coastal cliffs. Some of the flatter wet commons have open water and on their waterlogged soils grow wet heath plants and even fen and marsh species.

As one would expect, amphibians are common in the wetter areas and common frogs, common toads and palmate newts have been recorded at several of the

commons. These, in turn, attract a range of predators who live in or hunt over these areas. Grass snakes, for whom amphibians are a major dietary item, are found here. Foxes, badgers, hedgehogs, mink and even the occasional polecat pass through from time to time in search of food and their tracks and signs may be seen.

Semi-aquatic mammals also inhabit these wetter areas. Water voles have been recorded near Trewellwell, and they breed downstream at Middle Mill. Water shrews live at some of those commons adjacent to the River Alun, although a diving body or a trail of bubbles in the water may be all you see of one.

Other species you may come across include common lizard, adder, common shrew, mole, rabbit, wood mouse, bank vole, house mouse, brown rat, grey squirrel and weasel.

30 LLANBORTH FARM

LOCATION *Dyfed*; immediately north-west of the hamlet of Penbryn, 2 miles east of Aberporth.

This small National Trust property on the Dyfed coast is extremely varied. Two pieces of woodland are included consisting mainly of sycamore and ash, one of which has a stream running through it, bounded by alders. Where these woods run out to the cliff top, there is an area of scrub and bracken which provides excellent cover for mammals.

Badgers are found here and foxes lie up here too and include the beach in their foraging area. Look for their four-toed tracks walking an imaginary tightrope in the sand. Also, keep an eye open for signs of stoat, mole, common shrew, rabbit and field vole.

31 CROFT CASTLE

LOCATION *Hereford and Worcester*; 5 miles north-west of Leominster, 9 miles south-west of Ludlow.

Croft Castle is a sizable estate of historical significance – its parkland is thought to date from the 17th century. Within the grounds are the remains of an Iron Age hill-fort at Croft Ambrey from where there are good views to the north and west. The estate also has a Site of Special Scientific Interest within its boundaries, containing a number of species.

The string of ponds which have been formed along the stream to the north of the castle are a valuable habitat for amphibians. Frogs and toads occur here, and except during their winter hibernation and spawning time in the spring, they may be found in damp areas. Palmate and great-crested newts can also be seen from time to time. Great-crested newts are protected and must not be disturbed.

Keep a look out for adders, grass snakes, slow-worms, common lizards, hedgehogs, common shrews, pygmy shrews, moles, rabbits, wood mice, bank voles, field voles, brown rats, grey squirrels, badgers, foxes, fallow deer and muntjac deer. It is fairly easy to distinguish between the different deer, especially since the muntjac is only about half the height of a fallow deer. When alarmed, the muntjac lifts up its tail to show the white underside – perhaps as a warning to others – while the fallow deer has a long black, white-fringed tail which makes its rump distinctive. The muntjac buck has dark stripes on his face and the doe has a black triangular patch on her forehead. Muntjac fawns are born singly at any time of the year. Their spotted coats fade within eight weeks of birth.

32 CHADWICH MANOR ESTATE

LOCATION *Hereford and Worcester*; 4 miles north of Bromsgrove, at the south-west edge of Birmingham, astride the A38 road to Worcester. Access only by public footpath except at Highfield where there is a country park.

The Chadwich Manor Estate is managed primarily for agricultural purposes. The land consists of improved and unimproved pastures, arable fields, woodlands and a number of ponds. Most of the estate is not open for public access, although it is crossed by numerous footpaths and the northern part, including Segbourne Coppice, is part of Waseley Hill Country Park. Lickey Hill Country Park is also close by on the east side.

The woodlands are mostly oak and hazel athough sycamore is dominant in Segbourne Coppice. Grey squirrels may be seen here. They are diurnal animals and this makes them easier to watch. Try to find their 'tables', a stump or stone on which they perch to eat hazelnuts. They leave a pile of neatly halved shells when they have finished their meal. You may also spot areas of bark peeled from sycamore branches where squirrels have enjoyed the sweet sap beneath.

Muntjac have now spread to the Midlands. These tiny deer seem hardly larger than a hare at first sight. They leave dainty cloven-hoofed footprints in soft ground and they also spend much of their time in undergrowth. Their pathways into bramble patches are clearly visible.

Look out, too, for signs of badger, fox, mole, rabbit and mink. Common toads and frogs, palmate newts, weasels, field voles and common shrews are also present.

33 CLENT HILLS

LOCATION *Hereford and Worcester*; 3 miles south of Stourbridge, south-east of Hagley, north and east of the village of Clent.

This is a National Trust property which is leased almost in its entirety to Hereford and Worcester County Council for use as a country park. The two hills, Clent and Walton, contain a variety of habitats suitable for animals and this is reflected in the long list of species recorded for the area. Rough open grassland and bracken grow on the summits and upper slopes of the two hills and provide plenty of food and cover for hares and rabbits.

A number of small mammal species — voles, mice and shrews, for example — have been recorded here and the tangles of dead material at the base of the rough grasses hide their runways. Careful delving should reveal passageways in the grass and possibly droppings too. Listen intently for a high pitched chirping sound, a little like the noise of a grasshopper, which is made by shrews when they are in dispute, defending territory. A shrew cannot bear another's presence, except when mating.

The southerly aspect of some of the slopes is favoured by adders who emerge early to sunbathe before they slide off to hunt their food. You may also find a beautiful but fragile outer skin which has been shed by one of these snakes.

Other species which occur at Clent Hills are common frog, smooth newt, palmate newt, badger, brown long-eared bat, pipistrelle bat, fallow deer, muntjac deer, fox, hedgehog, mole, house mouse, wood mouse, brown rat, bank vole, common shrew, pygmy shrew, grey squirrel, weasel and stoat.

34 ERDDIG

LOCATION *Clwyd*; 2 miles south of Wrexham off the A525.
OPEN 17 Apr to 18 Oct: daily except Fri but open Good Fri 12–5.
ADMISSION Garden and Museum £1.00; children 50p.

Erddig is a lowland agricultural estate of almost 1,000 acres. The natural history interest is mainly to be found in the woodlands and ponds on the property and, to some extent, in the River Clywedog although, because this is rather badly polluted, its wildlife value is limited. Hafod Wood and four ponds are managed as nature reserves by the North Wales Naturalists' Trust.

There are 140 acres of woodland on the estate consisting mainly of beech, sycamore and oak. The high canopies of several of the individual woods are quite extensive and their understoreys include hazel, ash, guelder rose, hawthorn and privet. Look for signs of badger here, not only in the woods themselves but where their pathways cross into farmland when you may find their characteristic coarse black and white hairs caught in clumps on the barbs of wire fences. If you come across a badger hole, it will be on a slope, probably about a foot wide and on light, well-drained soil. Usually, a hole does not smell and has no food remains outside; there may be loose soil containing badger hairs on the ground, thrown out with discarded nesting material.

There are over 70 small ponds and wetland areas on the estate and these have populations of frogs and toads, together with both smooth newts and the protected great-crested newts. Moles, rabbits, foxes, grey squirrels, hares and water voles have also been observed at Erddig.

35 DOVEDALE

LOCATION *Derbyshire*; **4–7 miles north-west of Ashbourne, west of the A515. Access by footpath.**

The steep-sided, rocky and wooded valleys, open grassland and streams that make up Dovedale provide ideal habitats for a wide range of animals. Dovedale lies within the Peak District National Park and the main trees here are ash, together with an understorey of hazel, field maple, holly and other species. These provide a rich variety of food plants for herbivorous mammals.

Water voles and water shrews both live along the River Dove. Water voles frequently become accustomed to the presence of people and continue with their daily lives unperturbed. The large number of visitors who use the riverside path has made these small animals quite tame and the quiet watcher on the riverbank should be able to observe their activities fairly easily. Water shrews tend to be more wary and only the very skilled or the very lucky will see one swimming underwater, its dark coat silvery with tiny bubbles of air trapped under its fur. Young shrews leave the nest at about four weeks old. You may see a family in procession, with the mother leading and the young following behind. Each holds on to the one in front with its mouth.

There are caves in the limestone rock of Dovedale some of which may be used by whiskered bats for winter hibernation. You are most unlikely to see them, however, since they will hide themselves in tiny crevices well out of reach – remember that it is against the law to disturb bats wherever they are.

Stoats, too, are known to inhabit areas of this property. They are skilful hunters and are very secretive. You may be fortunate enough to see one running across open ground in search of suitable prey.

Other species to look out for are common toad and common frog, pygmy shrew, common shrew, mole, Natterer's bat, brown hare, rabbit, field vole, grey squirrel, badger and fox.

36 HARDWICK HALL

LOCATION *Derbyshire*; **6½ miles north-west of Mansfield; 9½ miles south-east of Chesterfield.**
OPEN Park open daily all year.
ADMISSION Car park charge to non-National Trust members 40p.

Hardwick Hall is a large parkland area – over 500 acres are open to the public and much of the land is a country park, which includes a good proportion of the best wildlife habitat. Water is a strong feature at Hardwick Hall. The River Doe Lea runs around the western boundary, there are two large ponds – Miller's Pond and Great Pond – and a series of smaller ones known as the Row Ponds, together with an old duck decoy. These are used by water voles and you should look for their holes, tracks and droppings or creep up to the bank and hope to see one feeding.

In the spring, common toads will use the deeper ponds for breeding. Look and listen for the adults as they gather to mate, in a chorus of croaking, the females laying a necklace of spawn. Great-crested newts have been recorded too. These protected amphibians also prefer deeper water and may be seen as they surface for air.

You may see other mammals including pipistrelle bat, house mouse, wood mouse, common shrew, field vole, fallow deer, rabbit, mole, grey squirrel and fox.

37 LONGSHAW

LOCATION *Derbyshire*; **about 2 miles south-east of Hathersage on the south side of the A625.**

Extensive areas of woodland are included in the 1,100 acres of Longshaw Estate with Padley Wood being the best known of these. This is a Site of Special Scientific Interest because it is an ancient sessile oak wood. Other woodlands on the estate consist of oak-birch mixtures and there are plantations of broadleaved and coniferous trees too. On the higher ground of Longshaw, which is a country park, are heath and acid grassland.

Padley Wood occupies the narrow steep-sided valley of Burbage Brook and, among the trees, large boulders lie on the slopes. Many of the smaller mammals of the Longshaw Estate, and especially of Padley Wood, have been identified from owl pellets. Common shrew, wood mouse and bank vole occur mainly in the woodland areas where they are able to make full use of their ability to climb trees. In the more open parts of Sheffield Plantation, field voles may be found. Look for their runs in the tangle of dead vegetation at the base of the rough grasses. Pygmy shrews are found on the more open heathland and often at remarkably high altitudes for such small mammals.

This appears to be a good area for bats. In particular, Daubenton's has been seen in the company of pipistrelle, flying low over the lake after sunset. Noctules have been noted in Hay Wood and Natterer's and whiskered are all known to occupy roosts nearby. Other species recorded here include palmate newt, common frog, common lizard, adder, water vole, rabbit, brown hare, red squirrel, grey squirrel, stoat, weasel, fox and badger.

38 HIGH PEAK

LOCATION *Derbyshire*; **hill area and national park in the Peak District of North Derbyshire.**

High Peak is the name given to the Derwent Estate, Edale and Hope Woodlands. Taken together, these three areas cover an enormous part of the northern Peak District. They all lie within or on the borders of the 'Dark Peak' or millstone grit area as opposed to the 'White Peak' areas to the south which are composed of carboniferous limestone. Much of this upland area forms a gently undulating plateau of unenclosed moorland which is managed for sheep and grouse. A good proportion is a Site of Special Scientific Interest.

At altitudes between 900 and 1,800 feet in areas of heather, mountain hares are found. They are an outpost of the Scottish species introduced in about 1880 and about a thousand individuals live here, especially on the Derwent Estate. They are probably easiest to see in the spring when they have not fully moulted their white winter coats and will be conspicuous against a background of brown vegetation after the snow has melted.

The Edale section of the property consists of a number of farms, together with some woodlands and Winnats Pass with its limestone grassland flora. Various small mammal species and their predators have been observed here. Look out for mountain hare, brown hare, rabbit, hedgehog, mole, common shrew, pygmy shrew, water shrew, red squirrel, grey squirrel, wood mouse, bank vole, field vole, water vole, brown rat, weasel, stoat, fox and badger together with common lizard, palmate newt, common frog and common toad.

39 FORMBY

LOCATION *Merseyside*; **dunes, foreshore and pinewoods west of the town, 11 miles north of Liverpool.**

The National Trust owns 450 acres of dunes and woodland between the Mersey and the Ribble estuaries just to the north of Liverpool. The woodland here consists of pines planted at the beginning of this century in an attempt to stabilise the dunes. The intention was to construct an esplanade along the coast but the attempt failed and now the mixture of Scots and Corsican pines forms the basis of a reserve for red squirrels. These are continental squirrels introduced years ago and are easily seen for most of the year except in very cold weather. The remains of pine cones, left after squirrels have eaten the seeds, are nearly always in evidence.

40 EAVES AND WATERSLACK WOODS

LOCATION *Lancashire*; **2-mile nature walk, 1 mile north-west of Carnforth.**

This property consists of over 100 acres of woodland lying within the Arnside-Silverdale Area of Outstanding Natural Beauty. The natural history interest of this woodland, which is growing on limestone paving, is so valuable that almost the whole area has been declared a Site of Special Scientific Interest. It is a mixed wood variously dominated by ash, oak and beech with a liberal scattering of larch, Scots pine and sycamore. In parts the understorey is of hazel and these areas are worth investigating for traces of wood mice and bank voles. Look for hazelnut shells with holes

gnawed in their sides. The methods used by these two mammals to extract the kernel are quite different and are a characteristic sign of their presence. You may even discover a wood mouse's winter store of nuts.

The woodland is grazed by both red and roe deer, and fallow deer are believed to pass through from time to time. You may be lucky enough to see any of these species, although deer generally lie up during the day, often in seemingly impossibly sparse cover.

You may also observe common toad, red squirrel, mole, rabbit and hedgehog.

41 CONISTON

LOCATION *Cumbria*; **6 miles southwest of Ambleside on the north and east sides of Coniston Water.**

This large and varied property lies within the Lake District National Park. It contains many well known features of the area including the much visited Tarn Hows, and Peel Island, in Lake Coniston, which is reputedly the island on which Arthur Ransome based Wild Cat Island in *Swallows and Amazons*. Its biological interest is reflected in the fact that five Sites of Special Scientific Interest are included within, or come close to, its boundaries. The Coniston property encompasses 22 woodlands and these are used by both red and roe deer. You may find their cloven-hoofed tracks in damp places and their droppings, which are shaped like miniature wine bottles. Look out too for lying-up places – small patches of ground scraped clear of vegetation where the deer sleep during the day. A typical clue is the presence of a few coarse white hairs which have a crimped appearance. You may even be lucky enough to see the deer themselves.

The areas of open grassland and grass heath, especially where they have a southerly aspect, are good places to search for common lizards. You may spot them sunbathing or scurrying off through the grasses and into cover at your approach.

Common frog and common toad, rabbit, red squirrel, wood mouse, common shrew, mole, stoat, weasel, fox and badger are also present at this site.

42 HAWKSHEAD AND CLAIFE

LOCATION *Cumbria*; 4 miles southwest of Ambleside and west of the northern half of Lake Windermere.

Claife forms the main block of woodland on this estate which lies on the north-western shore of Lake Windermere. There are 750 acres of woods here, much of them covered by Claife Heights Site of Special Scientific Interest. Also included in the property are Blelham Tarn and Blelham Bog. The former is another Site of Special Scientific Interest while the latter has been designated a National Nature Reserve by the Nature Conservancy Council. The lake shore adds to the variety of habitats.

Claife Woods consist of a broad mixture of deciduous species and are a fine example of an ungrazed native woodland. Notably there are good populations of both yew and small leaved lime. Roe deer are known to frequent the wood and are probably best seen in the early mornings and evenings in the surrounding fields and when they emerge from the woods to feed. Red deer also live in this area and you may see their much larger slots or hoof prints in the soft ground.

Another species to watch for in these northern areas are red squirrels and, as they are active by day, the observant naturalist should see them from time to time. Look out, too, for signs of moles in the woods. They inhabit woodland as well as fields but the dead leaves on the ground often hide their hills. Other species you may see include common frog, fox, badger, rabbit, wood mouse and bank vole.

43 AMBLESIDE AND TOWNEND

LOCATION *Cumbria*; 4 miles northwest of Windermere. Townend is at Troutbeck, 3 miles south-east of Ambleside.

The various segments of this property are centred around Skelghyll Wood on the north-eastern shores of Lake Windermere. In addition to the wood, which contains the viewpoint, Jenkin Crag, there are a number of rough pasture fields, some of them running down to the lake shore. These pastures may be poorly drained in parts while rock outcrops, often featuring trees, add further interest.

The best section of the National Trust ownership for mammals is Skelghyll Wood. The quiet walker may see red squirrels feeding in the trees or, with even more careful fieldcraft, come across a solitary roe deer. Brown hares occur here. While they are generally considered to be animals of open fields, hares do use woodlands extensively, especially in these northern areas where the weather can be hard. At such times, woods provide shelter and food when the grass outside the wood is thick with snow. You may find their paths leading in and out of the wood and an early morning walker may see the animal returning to its daytime form.

Other animals to be found here include common shrew and pygmy shrew, mole, rabbit, wood mouse, bank vole, field vole, badger and pipistrelle bat.

44 WETHERAL WOODS

LOCATION *Cumbria*; on the left bank of the River Eden, just south of Wetheral, 5 miles east of Carlisle.

Wetheral Wood follows the outside of the curve of the river as it bends. The predominant tree species in the wood is wych elm although some large oaks are present, together with ash, sycamore and hazel. The last provides one of the food sources in the autumn for the red squirrel which has been recorded here. Look for its feeding signs and dreys, its tracks in muddy ground and for the delightful animal itself. Hedgehogs have also been seen in the woods and you may come across their tracks in mud and their characteristic black droppings.

Winter is often a good time to visit a wood like this. Snow enables you to follow the tracks of many species and to get a much clearer idea of their activities than would otherwise be the case. You may also come across water vole, mole and roe deer. You will not see hedgehogs in winter because they hibernate in weatherproof nests, often at the bottom of a hedge. Dead leaves are the best material for building a nest. The hedgehog carries the leaves to its chosen site and piles them in a heap supported by brambles or brushwood. It burrows into the heap and shuffles around until the leaves are all firmly packed into the walls of the nest. When hibernating, the hedgehog's body temperature drops and it will remain inactive until warmer weather returns.

45 CRAGSIDE

LOCATION *Rothbury, Northumberland*;
15 miles north-west of Morpeth.
OPEN Country park Apr to end Sept:
every day 10.30–6. Oct: every day
10.30–5. Nov to end Mar: Sat and Sun
10.30–4.
ADMISSION Country park £1; children 40p; pre-arranged parties 70p.

The land at Cragside was bought in 1864 by Lord Armstrong, the famous inventor and industrialist. Here he planted several million trees to create a retreat where he could combine his experimental and industrial interests with natural history and farming. On the 900 acres, Armstrong grew a broad range of imported coniferous trees together with native hardwoods. Some of the tallest trees in Britain grow here.

Water features strongly at Cragside. A number of lakes have been created including Tumbleton Lake, The Tarn and Nelly's Moss Lakes. Blackburn Lake has shrunk and is now a marshy wild area and ideal habitat for frogs. Both the Debden Burn and the Black Burn run through the estate, tumbling over waterfalls and through cataracts.

Bats are known to roost on the estate. Long-eared and pipistrelle have been recorded here, together with a single Leisler's bat. Daubenton's bats have also been seen feeding over the lakes and may roost on the property.

Roe deer are numerous in this part of Northumberland and the estate at Cragside is no exception. A quiet walk along the 40 miles of carriageways and drives may enable you to catch a glimpse of one of these small and generally solitary deer. You may also see red squirrel, fox, badger, rabbit and adder.

46 FARNE ISLANDS

LOCATION *Northumberland*; 2–5 miles off the coast, opposite Bamburgh.
OPEN Apr to mid May and mid July to end Sept: daily 10–6. During the breeding season (mid May to mid July) access is restricted: Staple 10.30–1.30, Inner Farne 1.30–5.
ADMISSION Mid May to end July £2.40. School parties £1.00. At other times £1.60; school parties 60p. Fees do not include boatmen's charges.

There are some 30 islands in the Farnes' group covering 80 acres but only two of the largest – Inner Farne and Staple Island – are open to the public. They are reached by motor boat from Seahouses on the Northumberland coast and were made famous by Grace Darling, the lighthouse keeper's daughter, who carried out a daring rescue, helping her father to save five people from a wrecked steamer in 1838.

The islands are best known among naturalists for their large populations of sea birds which come to the Farnes in the spring to breed. For the mammal watcher, though, grey seals are the attraction. Almost 6,000 seals come here to breed in the late autumn and may spread over whole island system. They are present throughout the year and have become accustomed to the regular appearance of the motor boat bringing visitors.

In the wet, misty days of autumn grey seals come ashore to their breeding grounds, normally to the same place year after year. The big bulls arrive first to establish territories above the high-tide line. The biggest bulls, the beachmasters, have the most extensive territories and the largest harems – about ten or more cows – so they father the most pups.

The cows come ashore a few days after the bulls and are ready to give birth from the previous season's mating. They join a harem, not necessarily with the same bull each year, and are jealously guarded while they have their single pup because they are ready for mating soon after giving birth. Implantation of the fertilised egg is delayed for about three months so that a cow will not give birth before the following autumn.

A pup will feed on its mother's rich milk every five hours for three weeks. During this time, the pup triples its 32 lb birth weight, but the cow cannot go out to sea to feed. Instead, she will defend the area around her own pup and will fiercely repel intruders, including other pups, with bared teeth, hoots and threatening lunges. After about two or three weeks, the pup sheds its creamy-white baby coat and becomes pale grey. When her pup reaches this age, a cow will go to feed as the tide rises. When she returns from feeding, she finds her pup first by recognising the place, then picking out its voice and finally by sniffing at the pup to check its scent. A bull, however, dare not desert his territory, so he will live off his fat for nearly eight weeks.

When pups are two months old they are ready to go out to sea. Once they are weaned and have left the breeding beaches, they do not return for several years until they are adult. Cows mature at four or five years old; they come ashore to breed every year until they are about 35 or more. Bulls may mature at about six years old but are not big enough or strong enough to gain and defend a territory until they are at least nine. Then they breed every year for about four or five seasons, but become worn out with the strain. Few bulls survive beyond about 20.

Deer parks in England and Wales

The earliest deer parks were enclosed areas kept for hunting by the king and his lords – in much the same way as the Royal Forests, although these were not enclosed. Smaller deer parks were used as living larders and were maintained, as were rabbit warrens, for keeping meat 'on the hoof' until it was required in the kitchen. In the days before refrigerators the only way to preserve meat for winter was to salt it, so that by the early spring it was often in a very poor state and fresh venison was a great luxury.

Captive deer herds were often augmented from wild stock inhabiting the surrounding countryside. By arranging the park fencing so that the ground level was high on the outside but low on the inside, wild deer could be encouraged to use this 'deer leap' to spring nimbly into the park and join the animals there, only to find that subsequent escape was impossible. This arrangement may have been the predecessor of the ha-ha, an 18th-century adaptation of the idea, much used in landscape gardening. During the 18th century, traditional parkland – consisting of permanent pasture with a scattering of standard trees – became the vogue. The ha-ha with its sloping ditch and vertical stone wall prevented any grazing stock from invading the garden around the house while allowing an unimpeded view of the parklands.

Today a number of large estates still have deer parks. The species most commonly found in parks are fallow, red and sika deer.

Looking for signs of deer

Trees in a deer park often have a distinct line where deer browse for accessible shoots – at the height the deer can reach to feed when standing on hind legs. Palatable shrubs such as hawthorn are often shaped strangely by deer browsing. Deer of any species can cause considerable damage to trees by fraying bark when they clean their antlers, by breaking branches when they thrash with their antlers at rutting time and also by stripping bark to eat. A tree's growth may therefore be distorted by deer and, if the bark is rubbed or stripped off all round, the tree may even die. This is why trees in a deer park are often protected by wooden palings. In commercial forests the damage can be serious and new plantations in traditional red deer areas are generally fenced off.

Deer seem to enjoy the taste of a salt lick, which provides them with minerals such as sodium, calcium and magnesium, and so these are sometimes fixed to a tree or stump.

Observing deer

Once they have moulted their winter coats – usually by May or June, depending on the species and the weather – deer have bright, glossy summer coats. Winter coats usually start growing in about September and are duller and thicker than summer coats. Species, such as fallow, that are spotted in summer generally lose their spots in winter, and most young deer change to adult colouring when they are a few months old. Several species are similar in colour and build but at all times of year the main identification points are the variations in rump pattern, tail markings and length and, in males, antler patterns.

Only deer grow antlers, which are quite different from horns, of cattle, for example although they are used similarly – mainly as weapons. Horns are permanent bony growths covered with a sleeve of horn, and occur in both sexes. Antlers are bony growths that drop off and are regrown every year but (with the exception of reindeer) only by the males. While antlers are growing they are covered by a hairy skin called velvet. Blood vessels in the velvet supply food and oxygen to the growing bone. When the antler is fully grown the velvet is shed or rubbed off and the antler dies, although it remains on the deer's head for several months. The pattern of the antler cycle is similar in all species, but times of casting and cleaning may differ. Most species in Britain shed their antlers at some time in the early spring or summer and have new ones fully grown in the late summer or autumn, before rutting time. Roe deer, however, shed their antlers in winter and have fully grown ones about April. With some species, each pair of antlers grown is normally larger and with more tines, or points, than the previous pair, until the deer reaches old age. A deer's age cannot be measured by the number of points it has, but they do indicate whether it is young or old.

Species commonly found in parks

Fallow deer are a pleasure to watch in any season and are most attractive animals with their rows of spots and interesting colour variations. Look for them in the parks, particularly in late June when most of the fawns are old enough to gambol together in the cool of the evening – playing in groups, chasing each other and jumping on and off grassy hillocks. Fawns spend much of the daytime trotting after their mothers and grazing, as well as being suckled several times a day, and many does suckle their fawns into the new year. All fawns rest for much of the day in the first week or two of life but if you see some resting in the grass while others play, these may be the late-born fawns.

Fallow bucks cast their antlers at any time from late March to early June. They spend summer in a bachelor group while new antlers are developing. When the antlers are fully grown – towards the end of August for older bucks – the soft covering, or velvet, is rubbed off against trees until they are clean and hard, ready for rutting in the autumn. Bucks live peaceably together in summer, separate from the does and fawns. They put on weight as they graze on the rich grass, and are in their prime in August and September – the 'fat buck' season. In winter, many park deer are provided with extra food, usually hay which is placed in racks or root crops such as swedes which are spread on the ground. From two years old a doe normally bears a fawn every year for perhaps ten years or more, and herds increase rapidly. To prevent overcrowding and disease and the destruction of their habitat, the deer are regularly culled (selectively killed); bucks from August to April, does from November to February.

For most of the year red deer live quiet and unobtrusive lives, but for about three weeks beginning in September, the countryside echoes to the stags' bellowing roars and clashing of antlers. This is the rutting season, the courting and mating time when the stags move into the areas where the hinds live. Stags are in their prime at the start of the rut, with hard, fully grown antlers, a thick neck and a heavy winter mane as well as plenty of fat reserves built up during the rich summer's grazing.

Each stag tries to round up a harem of hinds, but his success depends on his size, age and how impressive he looks at other stags. Generally stags try to avoid fighting and although intense and prolonged fights do occur, most are settled by a display of strength.

Although sika deer are less common in deer parks than fallow, you may see them occasionally. There are some herds at Knole Park in Kent, for example. Sika deer can live in coniferous woods but prefer mixed woods with areas of shrubby undergrowth and will frequently graze on nearby grassland. These deer have white rump hairs which they can flare when alarmed making the patch very conspicuous. It acts as a warning signal to others as the deer flees from danger.

In April or May you may catch sight of rival stags on their hind legs, boxing. This is their way of settling a dispute when one or both stags have cast their antlers. Calves are born in May and June. They have white spots at birth, but after a few months the spots disappear. During the rutting season the deer are moulting from summer to winter coats and the stag grows a mane that is present all winter.

Where to find deer

Deer Park	Location	Species
Attingham Park, Shropshire	4 miles south-east of Shrewsbury	fallow
Charlecote Park, Warwickshire	4 miles east of Stratford-upon-Avon	fallow, red
Dunham Massey, Cheshire	3 miles south-west of Altrincham	fallow
Dyrham Park, Avon	4 miles south of Chipping Sodbury	fallow
Fountains Abbey and Studley Royal, North Yorkshire	2 miles west of Ripon	fallow, red, sika
Knole Park, Kent	at the Tonbridge end of Sevenoaks, just east of the A225	fallow, sika
Lyme Park, Cheshire	2 miles south of Disley	red
Petworth, West Sussex	13 miles north-east of Chichester	fallow
Powis Castle, Powys	on the south edge of Welshpool	red, fallow
Tatton Park, Cheshire	3½ miles north of Knutsford	red, fallow
Waddesdon, Buckinghamshire	6 miles north-west of Aylesbury	sika

Scottish sites

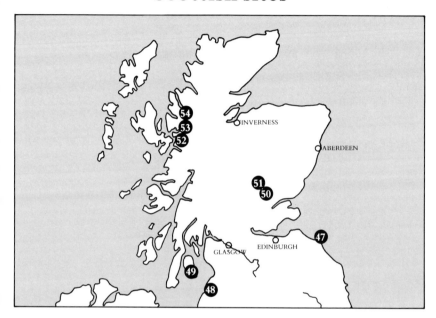

LOCATION *Strathclyde*; **4 miles west of Maybole.**

More than 250,000 people visit Culzean Country Park every year and yet an impressive number of species may still be seen within its 530 acres. Culzean lies on Scotland's west coast and the park's seaboard is a varied one. There are sandy bays, shingle and rocky beaches and extensive cliffs, especially around the castle. Grey seals may turn up here from time to time and you should carefully search the surface of the sea for the nose of a 'bottling' seal. The elusive and nocturnal otter also feeds along the coast here.

Inland, there are extensive areas of woodland and these harbour roe deer which have nearly become acclimatised to the presence of people. You may spot them more easily as a result and possibly have the chance to watch them for a little longer than usual.

Small mammals are plentiful. Both bank and field voles have been recorded at Culzean and a careful inspection around the bases of rough grasses should reveal their runs and possibly their nests and droppings. Other species recorded here include fox, polecat, stoat, weasel, mole, hedgehog, common shrew, brown rat, house mouse, wood mouse, water vole, red squirrel, brown hare, rabbit, pipistrelle bat, long-eared bat, common frog, common toad and common lizard.

If you see a lizard with a short tail, it is growing a replacement for one that it has shed. Sometimes a new tail grows beside one that is only partly lost, giving a double tail. Lizards also shed their skins periodically. If you see a lizard with a ragged appearance, it is in the process of moulting – the skin comes off in pieces.

47   ST ABB'S HEAD

LOCATION *Borders*; **rocky headland about 1 mile north of St Abbs.**

St Abb's Head is owned by the National Trust for Scotland and has been designated a National Nature Reserve by the Nature Conservancy Council. It is jointly managed with a Scottish Wildlife Trust. 190 acres in size, it contains a selection of different habitats. Rising from the bouldery beaches are cliffs 300 feet high, while offshore stacks are used by nesting sea birds. Inland, an old glaciated channel contains the man-made Mire Loch, which has treelined banks, gorse scrub and surrounding areas of grazed grassland.

A variety of animal species have been recorded at St Abb's Head in the past. You should see signs of moles here, but you will only find their hills where the soil is deeper because shallow areas are unprofitable for foraging moles. The long grassland in the Mire Valley contains many small mammals – bank vole, wood mouse, common shrew and water shrew – which will fall prey to the stoats seen frequently on the reserve. Both pipistrelle and long-eared bats occur here and pipistrelles have been recorded hunting over the water of Loch Mire. They feed mostly on gnats and tiny moths.

You may also see hedgehog, rabbit, hare, fox, mink, otter, grey seal and roe deer, if you are lucky.

49 BRODICK COUNTRY PARK

LOCATION *Strathclyde*; on the south-east coast of the Isle of Arran.

Behind Brodick Country Park, Goat Fell rises up to nearly 3,000 feet. The area around the castle consists of parks and gardens, grazing land and mixed woodland. The lower slopes of Goat Fell have been planted with large areas of conifers, while above these are the steeper heather-covered slopes. Close to the summit, the mountain becomes very steep.

A diverse selection of animals lives here. Along the coast there are grey seals, with their Roman noses and dog-like heads, and also common seals, whose appearance is altogether softer and more rounded. Pipistrelle bats roost in the buildings here and may be seen as they emerge at twilight, while red squirrels are fairly common in the garden areas as well as in the woodlands beyond.

Red deer may be seen here too. If you do not manage to spot these large mammals themselves, you may come across their tracks in the soft peaty ground or even a glutinous wallow created and used by the stags especially in the rut. A stag will wallow in mud until its body is completely mud-plastered. This helps to spread a strong rutting smell all over its body. Rutting stags emit deep, loud bellowing roars and they will try to outdo their rivals' roaring. You may see rival stags walking slowly beside each other, while they assess each other's strength before committing themselves to a fight.

Look out, too, for badger, mink, common shrew, pygmy shrew, water shrew, brown rat, house mouse, wood mouse, field vole, brown hare, long-eared bat, common toad, adder, common lizard and slow-worm.

50 THE HERMITAGE

LOCATION *Dunkeld, Tayside*; woodland just west of the town.

These 37 acres of woodland are just a little north of Birnam, whose wood was made famous by Shakespeare in *Macbeth*. The Hermitage is on the northern bank of the River Braan and is surrounded by land in the ownership of the Forestry Commission. It is a tree garden or arboretum and was planted in the 18th century by the Dukes of Atholl. Among the native trees are such peculiarities as the monkey puzzle and the cedar of Lebanon. The major tree species here include alder, yew, Douglas and silver fir, beech, larch, Scots pine and Norway spruce.

The variety of trees in these woods supplies a diverse habitat, which is especially good for small mammals. Listen for the high pitched, insect-like calls of fighting common shrews. Anyone more than about fifty years old may not be able to hear their battle cries but a bat detector, as used by bat enthusiasts to translate the ultrasonic calls of bats into audible sounds, can also be used to hear the calls of shrews when they are in dispute.

Roe deer use these woods, feeding here and in the surrounding areas, and lying up in cover during the day. Look for their lying-up places scraped clean of old leaves and other woodland debris. If you disturb a roe buck as it browses, it will bound unto the cover of trees – possibly clearing about 50 feet in one leap. When alarmed, roe deer fluff out the pale hairs on their rump, which looks like a large powder puff. Wary deer will often stamp their feet.

You may also see signs of mink, stoat, weasel, mole, wood mouse, field vole, red squirrel, mountain hare, rabbit, common frog, common toad and slow-worm.

51 LINN OF TUMMEL, THE PASS OF KILLIECRANKIE, AND CRAIGOWER HILL

LOCATION *Tayside*; south-east of Atholl, along the A9.

There are 54 acres of woodland at Killiecrankie where the River Garry passes through a gorge sufficiently narrow at one point – less than 20 feet – for at least one man to have jumped across it in the past, at the place known as Soldier's Leap. The riverside path leads to the Linn of Tummel, an anglicised form of the Gaelic, *Linne Tun Allt*. Here are 50 acres of riverside woodland dominated by Scots pine with some fine Douglas firs, larches and other softwoods together with oaks and sycamores. The third property, Craigower, lies a little further south to the east of the A9. It consists of a beacon hill 1,300 feet high, from the summit of which are fine views of the surrounding area.

An impressive range of animals have been recorded at these Trust sites. In particular, you should inspect the sandy beaches along the riverside for tracks as well as damp places in the woods themselves. You may come across the webbed footprints of otters or the delicate cloven-hoofed prints of roe deer.

Red squirrels live in the woods and the cores of cones will indicate the remains of their meals. Look for them, and listen for them too, as they scurry about in the tree tops seeking food or following their arboreal routes.

You should also keep an eye open for fox, mink, stoat, weasel, pipistrelle bat, rabbit, field vole, bank vole, water vole, wood mouse, pygmy shrew, common shrew, hedgehog, mole. red deer, common frog, common toad, common lizard and slow-worm.

52   BALMACARA

LOCATION *Highland*; 3 miles east of Kyle of Lochalsh.

The Balmacara Estate of over 5,600 acres includes almost the entire western end of the Loch Alsh peninsula. Kyle of Lochalsh, and the road to Skye, lies on the coast in the south-western corner and offshore there is a wide range of small islands, most of which are little more than rocks in the water covered with heather. They provide hauling-out places for common seals and you may see these mammals lazing on the rocks in the sun.

Inland, it is difficult to tell whether you are looking at islands surrounded by water or lakes bounded by land, there are so many lochs and lochans here. Away from the roads the country is wild and remote and is the habitat of many animals. Adders live here among the grass and heather, and prey on the many small mammals that also inhabit the area.

In sheltered parts the trees provide cover for roe deer and you may come across their tiny footprints in the soft peaty soil or see these small chestnut coated deer in the early morning or evening. Where there is little disturbance, roe deer will graze during the day and the quiet walker may surprise one doing just that. All deer like to browse on the brambles that grow in clearings and roe deer are especially fond of them. They will often feed on the tips of conifer shoots, but tend not to stand on their hind legs to reach them. In April, roes may damage trees by rubbing their antlers clean against the bark and branches.

You should also look out for fox, badger, otter, pine marten, stoat, weasel, mole, bank vole, field vole, rabbit, pipistrelle bat, frog, toad, common newt, common lizard and slow-worm.

53   KINTAIL

LOCATION *Highland*; mountainous tract in Skye and the district of Lochalsh, to the north-east of Glen Shiel.

The Five Sisters of Kintail, four of them over 3,000 feet high, are the focal point of this National Trust for Scotland Estate of more than 12,500 acres. These mountains rear steeply from Loch Duich and the energetic climber will be rewarded with wonderful views from their grassy peaks. Away to the north, at the end of an arm of the estate, lie the Falls of Glomach, one of the highest in Britain. The waters tumble from Ben Attow into the River Elchaig below, and from these to Loch Long. The warm climate here, although rather wet, is kind to wildlife which can find shelter in the wooded areas of this estate.

Red deer roam the hills, retreating to the high ground to try to escape the insects in the summer. Foxes, too, live in the corries remote from Highland shepherds and their terriers. Wild cats and pine martens are also here but so elusive that only the very fortunate will be lucky enough to see them. Wild goats scale the rocks on nimble hooves but you may have difficulty in distinguishing their footprints from those of sheep and deer where the peat is soft. The goats browse on shrubs such as gorse and heather, and will also eat leaves from trees – sometimes standing on their hind legs to reach a branch.

You may also see badger, otter, stoat, weasel, common seal, sika deer, roe deer, mole, common shrew, brown rat, house mouse, wood mouse, water vole, bank vole, field vole, mountain hare, rabbit, pipistrelle bat, frog, toad, newt, adder and common lizard.

54   TORRIDON

LOCATION *Highland*; large areas of nature reserve off the A896.

The enormous Torridon estate came into ownership of the National Trust for Scotland in 1967. It contains a number of the highest and best-known mountains in this area including much of Beinn Eighe, Liathach and Beinn Alligin. Immediately adjoining it is the Nature Conservancy Council's Beinn Eighe National Nature Reserve. Together the two owners jointly control an area 12 miles long and 4 miles wide.

The walker can leave the shores of Upper Loch Torridon, pass through the heaths and bogs of the lower ground and climb up to the more barren and almost bare rocky areas of the higher mountain sides. Here, where the mountains rise to almost 3,000 feet, wide rocky ledges in the sandstone support mountain plants, and screes and ravines have their own particular flora.

Open and sparsely populated localities such as this provide superb areas for so many of the wild mammals squeezed out of the rest of the British Isles by disturbance and a growing human population. Large numbers of red deer may be spotted, especially in hard weather when they come down to the lower ground through which roads run. Wild goats occur in the coastal parts while the occasional mountain hare inhabits the higher ground. Otters use both freshwater rivers and burns, and the sea. The fortunate and the patient may be lucky enough to see one.

Pine martens and wild cats are known to live here but, as they are both scarce and nocturnal, the chances of seeing either are small. Look out, too, for roe deer, sika deer, badger, fox, stoat and weasel.

Irish sites

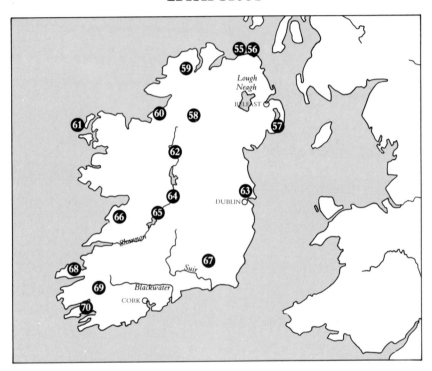

Lough Neagh

BELFAST

DUBLIN

Shannon

Suir

Blackwater

CORK

55 56
59
60 58
61 57
62
64 63
65
66
68
69
70
67

---

55   GIANT'S CAUSEWAY

LOCATION *Co Antrim*; **unusual rock formations on the coast north of Bushmills, off the B146.**

Although most people visiting this 100-acre property will do so to enjoy the sea views from one of the most dramatic parts of the Irish coast and to see the famous columns of basalt upon which so much of the region's folklore has been based, there is still much to interest the animal enthusiast.

A number of walks have been planned along the cliffs which lead the visitor to the geological landmarks such as the Giant's Gate and The Organ. The paths they follow wind in and out with the coastline and up and down the cliffs themselves. From them you may see signs of rabbits or even the actual animals. Do not be surprised if some of them are black for this seems to be a feature of the species in this area. Irish (mountain) hares may be spotted here too. They are often easier to watch than the brown hare because of their habit of grouping together a little

like rabbits. You may see them in the nearby fields at twilight.

Grey seals come to the more remote bays and a careful watch should be kept for these sea-mammals as you walk around the cliffs. Foxes and badgers have also been recorded here.

---

56   LARRYBANE AND CARRICK-A-REDE

LOCATION *Co Antrim*; **coastal site 5 miles north-west of Ballycastle, off the B15.**

These two properties, together with the outlying Sheep Island, amount to almost 100 acres and, although just over half a mile apart, they are joined by a footpath. There are chalk and basalt sea cliffs here, along with pasture, scrub and a disused quarry.

The scrub is dominated by hazel, with an intermingling of grey willow and blackthorn. Wood mice, in particular, make full use of the food these provide. You may find nutshells opened by these mammals or even an old winter store, sometimes numbering 300 shells or more. Foxes will lie up in thick scrub during the day, emerging in the evening to hunt down the hedgerows, pick along the tideline or seek worms and beetles in pasture fields.

Grey seals are resident here and the observant should be able to watch them fairly easily. In fine weather, seals will haul themselves onto rocks to bask in the sun, sometimes in large numbers. The very lucky may even spot common porpoises swimming off the coast. The following species have also been seen here: brown rat, rabbit, Irish (mountain) hare, stoat, pygmy shrew and pipistrelle bat.

57   CASTLE WARD

LOCATION *Strangford, Co Down*; on the A25, 7 miles north-east of Downpatrick.
OPEN Grounds open dawn until 1 hour after dusk all year round. Coastal path and countryside open all year.

This property covers almost 800 acres of the southern shore of Strangford Lough to the north-east of Downpatrick. The habitats here include pasture and woodland, some ponds, saltmarsh and unimproved grassland.

Coniferous woods have been planted here and small areas of deciduous woodland occur along the shores of the lough and close to the house. Badgers have been reported as using these from time to time in the past. The open parkland and pasture which make up almost all the remainder of the property have a population of Irish (mountain) hares. These are worth looking out for, especially at those times when they gather together in groups to feed. They are much less solitary than the brown hare in this respect.

Both the freshwater ponds and the lough itself are attractive places for semi-aquatic mammals and it may be that otters, previously recorded in Strangford Lough, come ashore at Castle Ward to use the ponds. The buildings at Castle Ward are also known to hold roosts of both long-eared and pipistrelle bats. It is neither possible nor legal to visit the bats in their roosts but you may be able to see these endangered mammals as they go off to hunt at twilight. All British bats eat insects, but the long-eared bat also feeds extensively on larvae that are resting on foliage. It hovers while it seizes its prey.

You may also see hedgehogs, pygmy shrews, foxes, stoats and rabbits.

58   CASTLE COOLE

LOCATION *Co Fermanagh*; 1½ miles south-east of Enniskillen on the A4.
OPEN Estate grounds open Apr to end Sept: dawn to dusk.

The Castle Coole estate's 400 acres contain a variety of habitats, with three notable lakes and several areas of woodland. Some of the latter are semi-natural and have been planted for their amenity value – others are either plantations, or marginal woody fringes. Some of the more interesting woods are dominated by oak, while in Killynure Wood the major species is beech.

Badgers are present in the woodlands and have left their unmistakable signs. Look for well-trodden paths which, at first sight, appear to be man-made. The continuation of such a path through a hole in a hedge or under a fallen bough will confirm, however, that these have been established by badgers.

Grassland covers some 225 acres of the property, and 175 acres of this are in permanent pasture. Some of this tends to be poorly drained and is marshy in parts. Probably the most interesting animal to be seen here is the Irish race of the mountain hare. This is a smaller, stockier animal than the brown hare and lacks a white top to its tail. It is known to congregate in groups, especially in the winter, and this happens here. The mixture of woodland and pasture seems to suit these animals and the Castle Coole estate has a good number of them. Irish hares usually stay brown all year. Whenever possible, the hares will supplement their diet with bilberry shoots, rushes and cotton grass and they regularly eat their own droppings.

Other animals to look out for are red deer, rabbit, grey squirrel and fox.

59   GLENVEAGH NATIONAL PARK

LOCATION *Co Donegal*; woodland and mountain area, west of Gartan Lough. Access is from the north-east end of the lake.

Glenveagh National Park is based on a long glaciated valley set in the heart of the mountains of north Donegal. Quartzite peaks rise above the gardens and woods of Glenveagh Castle, their thin soils supporting a poor vegetation by comparison. The estate was run as a deer forest for many years and the herd of red deer, mainly of Scottish origin, is still large. Escapees occur over much of Donegal and into Fermanagh. The deer can be seen on the moor grass and blanket bog of the mountain slopes and less easily in the woodlands. Particularly in winter their grazing hinders tree regeneration and fosters the spread of rhododendron though steps are being taken to reverse this trend.

Often deer will also strip bark to eat from trees and they can break branches by thrashing their antlers against them during the rutting season. As a result of the damage the deer can cause, traditional red deer areas are generally fenced off in new plantations – especially in forests that are run on a commercial basis.

With the taller growth of cover on the woodland floor, wood mice and hedgehogs are now more abundant than they used to be. Look out for the caches of hazelnuts that the mice feed on and the single black droppings of the hedgehog. The wood mouse eats seeds and berries as well as hazelnuts and you may come across one hiding somewhere high up to escape predators while it is eating. The mice are good climbers and will sometimes take shelter in disused birds' nests.

60 GLENADE

LOCATION *Co Leitrim*; a cliff-walled valley slicing through the limestone Dartry Mountains.

Excavated and made sheer by moving ice, the cliffs have produced vast screes which slope down to the valley floor, and at one point into Glenade Lough. The screes are now largely grass-covered and are the preserve of sheep and rabbits, but loose rock and gashes at the base of the cliffs show that erosion is still active. Stoats live here, finding perfect homes among the rocks and plenty of food where rabbits are common. Their curiosity may lead a whole family to peer at the observer from different crannies. Above the cliffs, blanket bog stretches over the flat summits and the Irish (mountain) hare is frequently seen. You may surprise a fox lying up in the heather or searching for carrion. There are otters, too, in Glenade Lough.

61 INISHKEA NORTH

LOCATION *Co Mayo*; island off the west coast. Access by boat from Blacksod Bay.

A low reef of gneiss, Inishkea is more exposed than many Irish islands. During storms, seaspray blows over the entire island and the short grassland includes many maritime species, especially the sea and buck's-horn plantains. A few deserted houses huddle on the eastern side of the island, rather fewer than on Inishkea South which was the home of one of Ireland's two whaling stations in 1892. The grass is mainly grazed by sheep and barnacle geese.

The north end of the island is built of a storm beach of gigantic boulders which give a sense of the power of the sea. It is here that grey seals gather in large numbers in October to calve and later to mate. As one looks down on the animals from the rest of the island, it sometimes seems that the rocks are moving to the accompaniment of hoots and barks. Numbers of seals vary here and marking has suggested that some of them are an overflow from the Scottish colonies.

Other mammals on the island are rabbits and wood mice although there are neither trees nor many bushes for shelter. Standing on the cliffs, you may be lucky enough to glimpse a whale out to sea.

62 UPPER SHANNON

LOCATION *Co Leitrim*; west of Dromod off the N4.

Most Irish rivers hold otters and the Irish population of these animals is in fact the largest in Europe. Watching otters is seldom easy but the rewards for patience can be great. The Upper Shannon has all the right conditions for otters – slow waters with abundant fish, trees that grow on the riverbank and fall, trailing in the water, reedbeds for cover and little human disturbance. If you travel by boat, look out on the quieter peninsulas and islands for flattened tracks in the reed beds entering or leaving the water, droppings (spraints) in conspicuous places and feeding remains of fish-scales and bones.

Otters are partly active by night but the mink is likely to be seen in daylight exploring the river banks and piers or struggling through the water with food for its young. Although a relative newcomer, the mink is still extending its range

in many parts of Britain and Ireland. The river's insect life attracts many bats in the evening: pipistrelles, with their swift, twisting flight, are frequent and you may also see Daubenton's bats, distinguishable by a straighter flight pattern. At this time badgers will be coming out of their setts and the young ash in Derrygrasten Wood gives good cover for watching them. By day you can check what kinds of food they have been digging for – wild garlic, pignut or cuckoo pint.

63 BULL ISLAND

LOCATION *Co Dublin*; in the north part of Dublin Bay.

The Bull Island is a sandspit that has grown in Dublin Bay within the last 200 years. It is a bird sanctuary, a golf course and a beach for the capital city, and it accommodates these disparate uses effectively. Sand dunes lie in ridges along the front of the spit extending it gradually out to sea while a flat saltmarsh covers the landward side, the resting place for many thousands of wildfowl when the tide covers their feeding grounds in the bay.

Almost all the plants and animals that now occur have colonised the island without the help of man. The Irish (mountain) hare is one of the most conspicuous, its russet coat contrasting with the greyish colour of mountain hares elsewhere. The hares feed on the dune grassland and saltmarsh and at low tide you can follow their tracks even out on to the mudflats as they move between feeding grounds or run to escape wandering dogs. In late winter, groups of about ten animals together may be seen while from March onwards, you may come upon the leverets born that spring.

These hares share the island with the rabbit, wood mouse, house mouse and pygmy shrew. The house mice are generally paler than elsewhere and once were claimed as a separate race. Look out too for the linear tracks of the fox crossing the sand dunes to scavenge on the beach in search of food.

64 MONGAN BOG

LOCATION *Co Offaly*; **on the north side of Fin Lough, between Ballynah-own on the N62 and the ruined monastery of Clonmacnois.**

Mongan Bog is a raised bog near the Shannon which has retained much of its original wetness despite adjacent turf-cutting. It is owned by An Taisce and as one of the very few bogs preserved intact, it well deserves a visit. On any bog, animal life is limited by the acidic nature of the habitat and the slow growth of vegetation.

Tracks made across the bog by the Irish (mountain) hare indicate its presence and it is not unusual for foxes to use the tracks too. The animals' droppings cause a noticeable fertilising effect and encourage the seeding of grasses from surrounding land. Eagles and harriers kill mountain hares, especially leverets (the young). The hares may also fall prey to buzzards or wild cats, but foxes are the main predators.

Frogs do not breed in the bog pools but later in the year they invade the area in large numbers, their colours matching the yellows and greens of the sphagnum moss. They are drawn by the abundant insect food and in turn feed the kestrels and long-eared owls. Pygmy shrews inhabit the drier islands of cotton grass, where the hares may also rest and breed.

65 PORTUMNA FOREST PARK

LOCATION *Portumna, Co Galway*; **conifer plantation south-west of the town.**

Portumna Forest is set on the fretted north shore of Lough Derg, the biggest of the Shannon lakes. The limestone bedrock is low-lying and belts of fen and reedswamp alternate with scrub and woodland.

Like many country estates, Portumna Castle kept a herd of fallow deer and these have flourished to such an extent in the new conditions created by forestry that their numbers now have to be controlled. Large groups still exist, however, and it is not uncommon at dusk to frighten a group of 30 to 40 deer which stream off through the trees in silent but hasty retreat. Their footprints and droppings show that they feed at the edges of paths and rides.

Portumna lies at the western edge of the still expanding range of the grey squirrel and here the two squirrels co-exist, the grey much less shy and easier to see. Other woodland mammals occur, including the pine marten, and you may be lucky enough to see mink in some of the smaller bays or foraging along the waveline.

66 THE BURREN

LOCATION *Co Clare*; **immediately south of Galway Bay, bare limestone hills lying between the N67 and the N18.**

The Burren is a rocky tableland with a largely underground drainage which includes many caves. Only one river flows on the surface from source to sea and the

Fergus, which drains most of the eastern Burren, disappears many times on its way to Ennis. Grassland and hazel scrub form most of the vegetation but there are many areas of bare jointed rock where the cracks, or grykes, carry all the plant and animal life.

The density of wood mice may be high in the grykes, particularly where hazelnuts are abundant. The animals live here out of the range of most predators except the stoat which is quite common. Where there is soil available for burrowing, rabbits graze along with the herds of feral and domesticated goats and cattle that treat the area like one big commonage.

But it is mainly for the pine marten that the eastern Burren is known. Nowhere else in the country are you more likely to see this mammal though that of course does not ensure success. Look for the pine marten in the planted forests such as Dromore and as it crosses the rocks or the road between patches of hazel scrub. A search of prominent places on dead logs, stones or paths may reveal its droppings. If you are caving, remember the lesser horse-shoe bat, the one that hangs like a fruit from the roofs of caves or houses. Pipistrelles haunt most farmyards where trees offer shelter to flying insects.

67 WOODSTOCK FOREST

LOCATION *Co Kilkenny*; **just south of Inistioge.**

An old estate set on the banks of the River Nore, Woodstock is now a public forest of spruce, Douglas fir and hemlock with many ornamental conifers close to the ruined house and broadleaved trees elsewhere. The plantations occupy the steep valley side overlooking the silent tidal river. A few outcrops show the underlying granite but elsewhere the soil and leaf litter is deep and, in autumn, it sprouts many different fungi.

The red squirrel exists here in great numbers and in many years practically every tuft of honey fungus is nibbled and every spruce cone stripped. The cut stumps of the trees are used as tables by the feeding squirrels and piles of cone scales build up on them. The woods contain fox and badger as well as the stoat and hedgehog. Walk quietly along the river path and you may see the telltale V-ripple of an otter or meet a mink exploring the bank. In the evening, the air is full of bats which roost in some of the estate buildings. Look for the pipistrelle and long-eared bat.

68   LOUGH GILL

LOCATION *Co Kerry*; lake on the Castlegregory peninsula.

Lough Gill is a shallow lake enclosed by the two ridges of sand dunes that come together to form the peninsula. The grassland runs into the lake with a few rushes on the west and east sides but, to the south, there is extensive reed swamp with an interesting flora.

Lough Gill is listed as the easiest place to see natterjack toads. Listen for them croaking on May and June evenings or look for their strings of spawn caught among the waterplants. At other times of the year, frogs are more likely to be seen and there may be some newts.

Lizards live on the warmer parts of the sand dunes, particularly to the west of the lake. They will take full advantage of any slight bank or rise which will both give them shelter and tilt their recumbent bodies towards the sun.

69   KILLARNEY NATIONAL PARK

LOCATION *Killarney, Co Kerry*; large areas of lake shore, oakwood and mountain south of the town, off the N71.

The Killarney National Park contains most of what is best in the scenery and wildlife of Kerry. The country's largest natural woodland lies in a lake-filled valley surrounded by spectacular mountain peaks. The sharp sandstone ridge of Carrauntoohil looks down on the more rounded glaciated hills below with the limestone shores of Muckross Lake and Lough Leane further away. Abundant moisture and warmth encourage a distinctive southern element in the flora and fauna, reminiscent of Spain and Portugal or the Canary Islands.

Ireland's only native herd of red deer occurs at Killarney. The herd is split into mountain and lowland groups and to hear the stags roaring in October as the mists rise from Mangerton Mountain or from Lough Leane is unforgettable. In the deeper woodland the sika deer has multiplied alarmingly since it was introduced in 1865 and now exerts considerable pressure on the trees – including yew – and ground flora. Other mammals abound: the badger is especially numerous and you may come upon a fox, a stoat or a hare on almost any path. Otters feed in the larger rivers and secluded parts of the lakes, while the red squirrel is quite common.

Look out for lizards sunning themselves on rocks around Muckross Lake and listen for the angry squeaks of pygmy shrews threatening each other in the undergrowth. The bank vole has arrived in the park within the last 15 years, following its introduction in Limerick.

70   GLENGARRIFF

LOCATION *Glengarriff, Co Cork*; north-west and south of the village, off the N71.

Glengarriff lies on the edge of Bantry Bay – a long, enclosed sea inlet with the mildest climate of any part of Ireland. Oak forests and coniferous woods are strung out in a broad valley underneath the Sugarloaf Mountain where tipped beds of old red sandstone stand out like ribs through the blanket bog. A tumbling river descends through the forest and otters play in its deeper pools. But there are quieter places too: boggy clearings in the woods where the hum of insect life feeds flycatchers by day and bats by night.

The woodlands hold sika deer, badger and fox while hedgehogs may sometimes feed on the famous Kerry, or spotted, slug. Offshore the islets around Garinish Island are the calving places for up to twenty common seals. In July you can see adults and pups lying out on the seaweed-covered rocks, their coats varying from dark grey to brownish and olive green. The otter frequents the same sheltered bays but it requires a lot more luck to see this rare creature.

Conserving and protecting wildlife

Britain's wildlife is under threat, not so much from hunters and collectors, whose actions are strictly controlled by law, but mostly from the loss of shelter and living space, from poisonous insecticides and factory effluents, and from litter such as cans that may trap or wound animals.

Animal habitats are constantly being destroyed to make way for agricultural and building developments. This not only robs many small mammals and amphibians of living space but depletes the supply of insects and plants they depend on for food.

To help animals to survive, national and local nature reserves and forest reserves have been established, and some species, such as the sand lizard, are rare outside such reserves. The protection of caves and old mines where bats hibernate offers secure places for threatened species to live, as does the establishment of otter havens.

Other action that aids survival includes the provision of subways for badgers under roads and railways, and of escape ramps for hedgehogs and other small mammals in cattle grids. Also, warning signs for motorists are now sometimes posted on roads where frogs and toads cross in numbers to reach breeding ponds in spring.

How you can help animals

Apart from supporting or helping organisations working for wildlife conservation, there are a number of things you can do to help animals.

Do not litter the countryside. Every year thousands of animals die trapped in bottles or cans carelessly thrown away. Clear up bottles and cans, and pick up plastic bags and cartons, which may be swallowed by deer or ponies and cause them to choke, or may suffocate animals that investigate them or try to nuzzle food from them.

Leave somewhere for animals to live. Paradoxically, too much tidiness can be as harmful to animals as carelessness with litter, because clearing out garden corners, grubbing up shrubs and mowing roadside verges destroys the living space of many small creatures. Try to tolerate selective untidiness. A pile of leaves left in a sheltered corner may provide somewhere for a hedgehog to hibernate. A piece of corrugated iron or similar material left in a grassy spot may become a nesting place for voles and wood mice. In a sunny place it enables reptiles to bask underneath, hidden from predators.

Avoid the excessive use of garden chemicals. Insecticides and slug pellets used too liberally may kill far more creatures than those that are damaging flowers or crops.

Britain's lost beasts

Many animals that were once common in Britain and Ireland are no longer found here. Some died out in comparatively recent times. With the development of farming and the loss of wild country, there was simply no room for them to exist alongside the spreading human population. Others were inhabitants of Britain in the long-distant past when the climate was either tropical or in the throes of glaciation. They fell victim to the changes in climate.

Bears and wolves roamed free in Britain until several hundred years ago. Brown bears were common during Roman times, and many were exported for use in wild beast shows. But they had died out by the early Middle Ages, killed by farmers who were concerned for the safety of their flocks and herds. They still persist in parts of western Europe, although they are now rare.

Wolves survived in England until about 1550, and small numbers were still to be found in Scotland and Ireland in the 1700s. Place-names such as Wolf Hole Crag in the Forest of Bowland in Lancashire recall their former moorland and mountain haunts.

Other large carnivores once native to Britain were the glutton (or wolverine) and the lynx. They probably died out in Britain during the Stone Age, some 5,000 or more years ago, but still exist in North America and the Arctic, the lynx also in a few remote parts of Europe.

Wild boars were once widespread in Britain, but died out here in the 17th century. Animals of the open woodlands, they gradually disappeared as forests were felled, and they were also relentlessly hunted for food and sport. They are still common in heavily forested areas of continental Europe.

Britain's beavers were once prized for their valuable fur and also their musk glands, which were believed to have medicinal properties. There has been no evidence of beavers in the wild in Britain since the 12th century, but they are recalled in place-names such as Beverley in Humberside. The beaver is still found in other parts of Europe, but is very rare.

Many small mammals and amphibians (birds, too) rely on insects as a food supply. The accumulation of poison from contaminated insects can lead to the death or decline of creatures that eat them, such as hedgehogs or bats.

Create habitats for various animals. Several species can be helped by building them a suitable habitat, and this also offers you a chance to study them. A grassy, undisturbed corner of the garden where the vegetation is left untouched will encourage butterflies and perhaps small mammals as well.

A garden pond will often attract frogs, toads and newts, and they will help to keep down insect pests. Bird nest-boxes will sometimes be used by squirrels and dormice. Boxes with an entrance at the base can be fixed to a tree or wall to attract bats.

How the law protects wildlife

To keep Britain's wild animals free from being harmed or disturbed by people, most are protected by law. Species that are endangered and declining in numbers are given full legal protection. They are:

Otter	Sand lizard
Red squirrel	Great crested newt
Bats (all species)	Natterjack toad
Smooth snake	

This means that it is against the law to:
● Kill, injure, sell, capture or keep them (even for a short time for marking).
● Disturb them in their breeding sites and places of shelter. Disturbing does not refer just to touching or moving the animals, but also to photographing them or doing anything that alarms them or rouses them from hibernation.
● Destroy or damage their breeding sites or places of shelter, or block the ways in and out of them.

Although badgers are not rare or endangered, the same protection applies to them, except where there is licensed control of numbers. It is also against the law to ill-treat a badger.

The accidental killing or injury of a protected animal is not a breach of the law. If you find an injured animal of a protected species, you are allowed to keep it and take care of it until it can fend for itself again. If it is too badly hurt to recover, it may be humanely killed without breaking the law.

Animals partly protected

Although it is not against the law to kill or capture animals that are not fully protected, there are strict regulations regarding the methods that may be used. Certain animals – the polecat, wild cat, pine marten, common dormouse and fat dormouse, hedgehog, common, pygmy and water shrews – may not be caught or killed in traps or snares. Nor may they be killed or captured by the use of poisons, gas, lights, sound recordings or electrical devices.

Certain cruel or indiscriminate methods are forbidden for the capture or killing of any wild animal. They include the use of self-locking snares, explosives (apart from firearm ammunition) and live decoys. Weapons such as longbows and crossbows are also forbidden. Permitted types of snare must be inspected at least once a day to see if an animal has been caught.

Native species of amphibians and reptiles (in addition to those that are fully protected) may not be offered for sale without a licence. They are the common (or grass) frog, common toad, common (or smooth) newt, palmate newt, common (or viviparous) lizard, slow-worm (or blind worm), grass (or collared or ring) snake and adder (or viper).

Animals given seasonal protection

Seals are fully protected only during the breeding season. For common seals this is during the whole of June, July and August and for grey seals during the whole of September, October, November and December. At any time of the year, seals cannot be killed without a licence.

Deer are also seasonally protected, generally during the summer months, but close seasons vary with species. Females are usually protected for a longer period of the year than males. The close season dates in Scotland differ somewhat from those in England and Wales.

Dealing with bats in the house

Many of Britain's bats roost in buildings, often in modern houses, so they are the animals most likely to be disturbed by man. It is against the law, however, to get rid of bats from the non-living areas of your house – attics for instance.

Bats will not damage your property. They do not gnaw wood or bring in nesting materials, and bats' dry, powdery droppings, which consist mainly of insect fragments, are not a danger to health. A single bat may eat more than 3,000 insects on a summer's night, including crop pests and wood-boring insects.

Occasionally a bat may enter the living areas of your house. Even there you may not kill or harm it. Usually it will find its own way out if a window is left wide open. If a bat seems unable to find its way out or appears too drowsy to fly, lift it gently and put it outside on a wall or tree. Be sure to put on heavy gloves before you handle it; a frightened bat might bite, and a large one can give a painful wound.

Bats may be found hibernating in a cool cellar or outhouse during winter. Avoid arousing a hibernating bat, because it may die if it leaves the roost in winter.

Index

Acknowledgments

Wild animals is based on the Reader's Digest *Nature Lover's Library Field Guide to the Animals of Britain* to which the following made major contributions:

Principal consultant Dr Pat Morris
Other consultants Lawrence Alderson M. A. (Agric); Dr Trevor Beebee; Norma Chapman B.Sc., M.I.Biol; Dr Stephen Harris.

Artists Peter Barrett; Dick Bonson; Jim Channell; Kevin Dean; Brian Delf; Sarah Fox-Davies; John Francis; Tim Hayward; Rosalind Hewitt; H. Jacob; Robert Morton; David Nockels; Eric Robson; Jim Russell; Gill Tomblin; Libby Turner B.A.Hons; Phil Weare.

Cartography The distribution maps of animals are based on information supplied by The Biological Records Centre of The Institute of Terrestrial Ecology, and were prepared by Clyde Surveys Limited, Maidenhead.

The publishers wish to thank the following for contributions and invaluable help towards producing *Wild Animals*:
Michael J. Woods (English, Scottish, Welsh and Northern Irish sites)
Roger Goodwillie (Irish sites)

Keith Alexander (Zoologist on the Biological Survey Team) and Katherine Hearn (Adviser on Conservation) from the National Trust.

The Royal Society for Nature Conservation

The National Trust
for Places of Historic Interest or Natural Beauty
36 Queen Anne's Gate, London SW1H 9AS

The National Trust for Scotland
5 Charlotte Square, Edinburgh EH2 4DU

An Taisce (The National Trust for Ireland)
The Tailors' Hall, Back Lane, Dublin 8

16-031-1